Math Go Figure...

150 Word Problems

Daily Problem Solving

Vocabulary Review

Writing Activities

Sopris West Educational Services • Longmont, Colorado

SO-BTZ-843

Copyright 2005 by Sopris West Educational Services.
All rights reserved.

ISBN 1-59318-179-5

Edited by Linda Bevard
Text layout and design by Tracy Katzenberger

07 06 05 04   6 5 4 3 2 1

Printed in the United States of America

Published and Distributed by

SOPRIS
WEST
EDUCATIONAL SERVICES

4093 Specialty Place • Longmont, Colorado 80504
(303) 651-2829 • www.sopriswest.com

240STU/3-04/BAN/10M/086

Acknowledgments

We are grateful to all of the people whose contributions of thought, time, and effort were invaluable in the development of *Math: Go Figure....* There are, however, three special people who must be thanked individually. Their steadfast interest and perseverance assisted us in making *Go Figure* a reality.

We appreciate **Suzanne McNamara**—Suzanne the Math Dog—for sharing so generously her keen mathematical mind, her insightful and detailed comments, and far from least, her remarkable computer skills.

We thank **Sarah Curry**, a practicing high school mathematics teacher, and her students, for reviewing and piloting *Go Figure* during the developmental stage and for offering many practical content ideas and suggestions for use in the classroom.

We recognize **Lynda McKelvey**, a former middle school mathematics teacher and our driving force at Sopris West, for believing from the beginning that *Go Figure* was an idea whose time had come. She understood the critical need for user-friendly problem-solving materials for middle and high school students and carefully guided the project to completion.

Ken Andrews

During his career in education, Ken Andrews has held the positions of teacher; principal; psychologist; curriculum and assessment developer; director of testing and evaluation; director of planning, research, and program evaluation; and, most recently, author, educational consultant, and researcher in the areas of teaching, learning, and increasing student achievement. He has devoted most of his professional life to learning theory and its application to efficient classroom instruction, and his contributions to educational research have resulted in the development of many innovative teaching methodologies, learning systems, and assessment formats and technologies. In addition to his work in the schools, he was founder and director of the nationally known Denver Diagnostic Teaching Centers, a unique model that has served as a guideline for similar centers throughout the country, and cofounder, with coauthor Diane Johnson, of The Learner's Edge, Inc., described below.

Diane Johnson

Diane Johnson is an accomplished teacher, principal, educational trainer, and author. She is a specialist in the areas of curriculum, instruction, and assessment development and implementation. During her career as an educator, she worked with students and adults of all ages and ability levels in all basic academic subjects. Her varied background includes living and working in Mexico and southeast Asia as well as throughout the United States. Most recently she cofounded, with Ken Andrews, The Learner's Edge, Inc., an educational consulting firm devoted to the research and development of achievement-oriented learning programs and materials.

Established in 1998, The Learner's Edge, Inc., is an educational consulting/publishing firm devoted to making quality educational materials and services available to the education community and the public. In addition to *Go Figure*, the firm has created more than a dozen successful teaching/learning programs, including *Little Words for Little People*, a beginning reading program for grades K–2; *Jump Start*, a series of reading programs for grade 3 through adulthood; *Think Sheets*, a reading comprehension/critical-thinking program; and *Reading Achievement at a Glance* and *Math Skills at a Glance*, standards-based performance assessments that sample typical skills and question formats found on most state standards assessments.

Contents

Welcome to *Go Figure*. The *Go Figure* program has been carefully researched and designed by a psychologist and an educator to assist teachers and students in the development of the critical-thinking and problem-solving skills required for success in today's math classrooms and on the most recent state assessments. The user-friendly approach of *Go Figure* gives teachers and students a basic framework to support and develop the ability to conceptualize and communicate mathematical concepts. *Go Figure* provides daily opportunities to investigate and apply problem-solving processes to a wide variety of math problems. It also gives diagnostic information about progress in a variety of mathematical areas. Successes and gaps in learning become obvious, providing an opportunity for timely acceleration or remediation when appropriate.

Go Figure samples universal content areas of accepted and widely used math textbooks and diverse math concepts and replicates local, state, and national math assessments. Problem-solving and critical-thinking skills that every student must know and be able to do are emphasized throughout. The program integrates the fundamentals of psychologically sound learning practices with a multisensory (visual, auditory, and kinesthetic) approach to learning that meets the needs of *all* learners.

Go Figure incorporates direct instruction and modeling with guided learning, independent practice, and the opportunity for the student to communicate the thinking required to solve a given problem. The instructional format is based on a supportive relationship between direct instruction and written application. Showing one's work and describing in writing the solution processes are essential parts of the program. Each problem integrates listening, observing, identifying key words, analyzing, deciding on a process, and showing one's work. Throughout the program there are abundant practice opportunities for independent application.

Each *Go Figure* problem has five distinct elements: **Think**, **Problem-Solving Plan**, **Solve**, **Communicate**, and **Vocabulary**.

1. **Think** introduces a problem designed to maintain and reinforce a variety of math skills. This section offers an opportunity for discussion, creativity, conceptualization, and the application of problem-solving skills.

2. The **Problem-Solving Plan** is a grid students use as a blueprint or checklist for solving problems. Students sequentially indicate the steps and strategies used to arrive at an answer. This diagnostic tool is a quick, reliable indicator of how a student thinks and manipulates information. Because strategies may vary, the plan is flexible and students may have different solutions. Students indicate the steps to a solution by entering sequential numbers (1, 2, 3 ...) (see example at right).

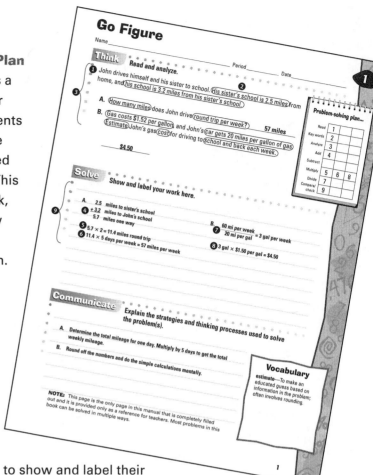

3. **Solve** requires students to show and label their work. Model responses appear in the Teacher's Guide; however, responses may be tailored according to teacher choice or teachers may accept other, valid individual student responses.

4. **Communicate** allows students to give a rationale for their solutions, explaining in writing the reasons for selecting certain problem-solving strategies. As above, model responses appear in the Teacher's Guide; however, responses may be tailored according to teacher choice or teachers may accept other, valid individual student responses.

5. **Vocabulary** presents and defines words pertinent to the solution of a given problem. On pages where no specific vocabulary appears, teachers and students may choose to introduce or reinforce important mathematical words or phrases.

Appearing periodically throughout *Go Figure* are **Try This** problems. These provide students with an opportunity to work independently. Performance on **Try This** allows teachers to know what each student can do and how each student applies previous knowledge to new and different math problems. No model responses are provided for **Solve** and **Communicate** for the **Try This** problems because answers may vary according to individual student interpretation and application. **Try This** is used according to teacher discretion and student readiness. Based on teacher judgment, however, any *Go Figure* problem can be used as a **Try This**.

Go Figure

Name_____ Period_____ Date_____

Think Read and analyze.

1 John drives himself and his sister to school. His sister's school is 2.5 miles from home, and his school is 3.2 miles from his sister's school. **2**

3

   A. How many miles does John drive round trip per week?   **57 miles**

   B. Gas costs $1.52 per gallon, and John's car gets 20 miles per gallon of gas. Estimate John's gas cost for driving to school and back each week.

      _____ **$4.50** _____

Problem-solving plan...

Read	1		
Key words	2		
Analyze	3		
Add	4		
Subtract			
Multiply	5	6	8
Divide	7		
Compare/check	9		

Solve Show and label your work here.

9

   A.   2.5 miles to sister's school
   4 + 3.2 miles to John's school
       5.7 miles one way

   5 5.7 × 2 = 11.4 miles round trip
   6 11.4 × 5 days per week = 57 miles per week

   B.   **7** $\dfrac{60 \text{ mi per week}}{20 \text{ mi per gal}}$ = 3 gal per week

   8 3 gal × $1.50 per gal = $4.50

Communicate Explain the strategies and thinking processes used to solve the problem(s).

   A. Determine the total mileage for one day. Multiply by 5 days to get the total weekly mileage.

   B. Round off the numbers and do the simple calculations mentally.

Vocabulary

estimate—To make an educated guess based on information in the problem; often involves rounding.

Go Figure

Name_____ Period_____ Date_____

Think **Read and analyze.**

Put these numbers in order from greatest to least.

0.004   0.65 $\frac{3}{4}$ $\frac{23}{5}$ $\frac{17}{6}$ 67% $1\frac{8}{9}$ $\frac{4}{5}$

_____
Greatest   **Least**

Problem-solving plan...

Read			
Key words			
Analyze			
Add			
Subtract			
Multiply			
Divide			
Compare/ check			

Solve   **Show and label your work here.**

Communicate   **Explain the strategies and thinking processes used to solve the problem(s).**

Vocabulary

This section may be used to introduce or reinforce any mathematical words or phrases.

_____
_____
_____
_____
_____
_____

Go Figure

3

Name_____ Period_____ Date_____

3

A. Identify these acute, right, and obtuse angles.

1.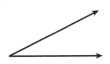

2.

3.

4.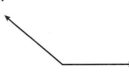

_____ _____ _____ _____

5.

6.

7.

8.

_____ _____ _____ _____

9. 96° = _____   **10.** 90° = _____   **11.** 125° = _____   **12.** 164° = _____

13. 40° = _____   **14.** 45° = _____   **15.** 37° = _____   **16.** 91° = _____

B. Draw and label an acute, right, and obtuse angle.

1.   **2.**   **3.**

_____ _____ _____

_____

_____

_____

_____

_____

_____

Vocabulary

acute angle—An angle that measures less than 90°.

right angle—An angle that measures 90°.

obtuse angle—An angle that measures more than 90°.

Go Figure

Name_____ Period_____ Date_____

Think — Read and analyze.

Vendria and William were in charge of stuffing bags with clown getups for the school carnival. Each bag contained a paper mask, a fake hairpiece, and a makeup kit. They sold 95 bags. Before filling the bags, they had 110 masks, 130 hairpieces, and 116 makeup kits. How many of each item did they have left after all the bags were sold?

_____

Problem-solving plan...

Read			
Key words			
Analyze			
Add			
Subtract			
Multiply			
Divide			
Compare/check			

Solve — Show and label your work here.

Communicate — Explain the strategies and thinking processes used to solve the problem(s).

Vocabulary

This section may be used to introduce or reinforce any mathematical words or phrases.

_____

_____

_____

_____

_____

Go Figure

Name_____ Period_____ Date_____

Read and analyze.

What would be the next two figures in the visual pattern below?

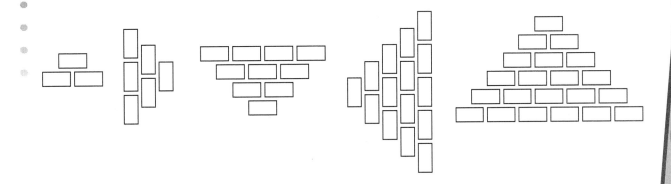

Communicate   **Explain the strategies and thinking processes used to solve the problem(s).**

Vocabulary

pattern–Figures, numbers, events, etc., that are arranged consistently according to certain identifiable variables.

Go Figure

Name_____ Period_____ Date_____

Think **Read and analyze.**

Put these numbers in order from least to greatest.

$\frac{3}{4}$ $1\frac{8}{9}$ $\frac{23}{5}$ $\frac{17}{6}$ 0.004 $\frac{4}{5}$ 0.65   67%

_____

Least   **Greatest**

Problem-solving plan...

Read			
Key words			
Analyze			
Add			
Subtract			
Multiply			
Divide			
Compare/check			

Solve **Show and label your work here.**

Communicate **Explain the strategies and thinking processes used to solve the problem(s).**

Vocabulary

This section may be used to introduce or reinforce any mathematical words or phrases.

Go Figure

Name_____ Period_____ Date_____

Think   Read and analyze.

To convert a percent to a fraction, drop the % sign, place the number over 100, and reduce the fraction to its simplest form.

Example: $75\% = \frac{75}{100} = \frac{3}{4}$

Problem-solving plan...

Read			
Key words			
Analyze			
Add			
Subtract			
Multiply			
Divide			
Compare/ check			

A. **1.** $20\% =$ _____   **2.** $50\% =$ _____   **3.** $45\% =$ _____

   4. $85\% =$ _____   **5.** $47\% =$ _____   **6.** $37.5\% =$ _____

   7. $64\% =$ _____   **8.** $87.5\% =$ _____   **9.** $40\% =$ _____

   10. $60\% =$ _____   **11.** $24\% =$ _____   **12.** $6\% =$ _____

B. In Ms. Green's class, 40% of the students lived within four blocks of the school, and another 50% lived between four and ten blocks from the school. What fractional part of the class lived within ten blocks of the school? _____

C. What fractional part of the class lived outside the ten-block area? _____

Solve

Show and label your work here.

Communicate   Explain the strategies and thinking processes used to solve the problem(s).

Vocabulary

percent—One part of a whole that has been divided into 100 equal parts.

fraction—A part of one whole unit. ($\frac{1}{2}$ = 1 of 2 equal parts; $\frac{3}{4}$ = 3 of 4 equal parts.)

simplest form— A fraction reduced to its lowest terms. ($\frac{3}{6} = \frac{1}{2}$; $\frac{5}{25} = \frac{1}{5}$)

Go Figure

Name_____ Period_____ Date_____

Think — Read and analyze.

Katie was learning to play golf. She played 18 holes of golf twice every weekend. Her scores over three weekends were 97, 100, 95, 89, 93, and 90. What was Katie's average, or mean, score?

_____

Problem-solving plan...

Read			
Key words			
Analyze			
Add			
Subtract			
Multiply			
Divide			
Compare/ check			

Solve — Show and label your work here.

Communicate — Explain the strategies and thinking processes used to solve the problem(s).

Vocabulary

average—The sum of the values of a set of items divided by the number of items.

mean— The sum of the values of a set of items divided by the number of items.

Go Figure

Name_____ Period_____ Date_____

Think — Read and analyze.

A. If smoked salmon costs $1.59 for a quarter-pound, what does a pound of smoked salmon cost? _____

B. How much would $3\frac{1}{2}$ pounds cost? _____

C. If you bought $3\frac{1}{2}$ pounds of smoked salmon and Cedric the hungry cat ate $\frac{3}{4}$ of a pound, how much salmon is left? _____

Problem-solving plan...

Read			
Key words			
Analyze			
Add			
Subtract			
Multiply			
Divide			
Compare/ check			

Solve — Show and label your work here.

Communicate — Explain the strategies and thinking processes used to solve the problem(s).

Vocabulary

This section may be used to introduce or reinforce any mathematical words or phrases.

_____

_____

_____

_____

_____

_____

Go Figure

Name_____ Period_____ Date_____

Think — Read and analyze.

If a garden is $4\frac{1}{2}$ feet wide and $6\frac{1}{2}$ feet long, what is the area of the garden?

_____

Problem-solving plan...

Read			
Key words			
Analyze			
Add			
Subtract			
Multiply			
Divide			
Compare/ check			

Solve — Show and label your work here.

Communicate — Explain the strategies and thinking processes used to solve the problem(s).

Vocabulary

area—The surface inside a closed two-dimensional figure or region.

Go Figure

Name_____ Period_____ Date_____

Think   Read and analyze.

To convert a decimal to a percent, move the decimal point two places to the right and add a percent sign (%).

Examples: 0.48 = 48%
              0.065 = 6.5%

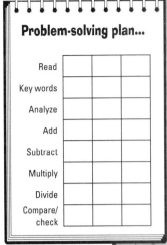

Problem-solving plan...

Read			
Key words			
Analyze			
Add			
Subtract			
Multiply			
Divide			
Compare/check			

A. **1.** 0.38 = _____   **2.** 0.075 = _____   **3.** 0.84 = _____

   4. 0.74 = _____   **5.** 0.375 = _____   **6.** 0.07 = _____

   7. 1.75 = _____   **8.** 1.25 = _____   **9.** 0.071 = _____

   10. 0.445 = _____   **11.** 0.010 = _____   **12.** 0.065 = _____

B. The lowest scores on the final test in the chemistry class were Ds. If 0.06 of the class received Ds, what percent of the class received higher grades? _____

C. At Dr. Kindheart's veterinary hospital, 0.53 of his practice involves dogs and 0.31 involves cats. What percent of his practice is devoted to other animals? _____

Solve   Show and label your work here.

Communicate   Explain the strategies and thinking processes used to solve the problem(s).

Vocabulary

decimal—Any base-ten number that names a whole quantity and a fractional part. The numeral(s) to the right of the decimal point indicate the fractional part.

percent—One part of a whole that has been divided into 100 equal parts.

Try This!

Name_____ Period_____ Date_____

Think and Solve   Read and analyze.

A. Identify these acute, right, and obtuse angles.

1.

2.

3.

4.

89° = _____

_____   _____   _____

5.

121° = _____

6.

7.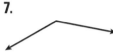

8.

_____   _____   _____

9.

14° = _____

10.

11.

90° = _____

12.

12° = _____

_____

13.

9° = _____

14.

15.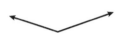

16.

179° = _____

_____   _____

B. Draw, label, and define an obtuse, right, and acute angle.

1.   **2.**   **3.**

_____   _____   _____

_____   _____   _____

_____   _____   _____

Communicate   Explain the strategies and thinking processes used to solve the problem(s).

_____

_____

_____

_____

_____

_____

Vocabulary

This section may be used to introduce or reinforce any mathematical words or phrases.

_____

_____

_____

_____

_____

_____

Go Figure

Name_____ Period_____ Date_____

Think   Read and analyze.

Rosa can buy 5 rugs at the flea market for a total of $116. She can sell them in her shop for $45.95 each. How many rugs must she sell to make a profit of $1,500?

_____

Problem-solving plan...

Read			
Key words			
Analyze			
Add			
Subtract			
Multiply			
Divide			
Compare/ check			

Solve   Show and label your work here.

Communicate   Explain the strategies and thinking processes used to solve the problem(s).

Vocabulary

profit—The amount of money gained in excess of the original cost.

14

Go Figure

Name_____ Period_____ Date_____

Think — Read and analyze.

Match these fractions with their equivalent percent values.

$\frac{2}{3}$ $\frac{7}{8}$ $\frac{4}{5}$ $\frac{1}{10}$ $\frac{2}{5}$ $\frac{3}{10}$ $\frac{3}{8}$ $\frac{7}{10}$ $\frac{3}{5}$ $\frac{9}{10}$ $\frac{5}{8}$ $\frac{1}{5}$ $\frac{3}{4}$ $\frac{1}{3}$ $\frac{1}{4}$ $\frac{1}{2}$ $\frac{1}{8}$

1. 25% _____
2. 20% _____
3. 50% _____
4. 40% _____
5. 60% _____
6. $33\frac{1}{3}$% _____
7. $37\frac{1}{2}$% _____
8. 10% _____
9. 90% _____

10. $12\frac{1}{2}$% _____
11. 70% _____
12. 30% _____
13. 75% _____
14. $87\frac{1}{2}$% _____
15. 80% _____
16. $62\frac{1}{2}$% _____
17. $66\frac{2}{3}$% _____

Problem-solving plan...

Read			
Key words			
Analyze			
Add			
Subtract			
Multiply			
Divide			
Compare/ check			

Solve — Show and label your work here.

Communicate — Explain the strategies and thinking processes used to solve the problem(s).

Vocabulary

fraction—A part of one whole unit. ($\frac{1}{2}$ = 1 of 2 equal parts; $\frac{3}{4}$ = 3 of 4 equal parts.)

equivalent—Equal in value; the same.

percent—One part of a whole that has been divided into 100 equal parts.

Go Figure

Name_____ Period_____ Date_____

Think **Read and analyze.**

Sherman's Computer Store has a computer on sale for $812.00. The sales tax is 7.5% (7.5 percent). What is the total cost of the computer? _____

Problem-solving plan...

Read			
Key words			
Analyze			
Add			
Subtract			
Multiply			
Divide			
Compare/ check			

Solve **Show and label your work here.**

Communicate **Explain the strategies and thinking processes used to solve the problem(s).**

Vocabulary

sales tax—An amount of money for government use added to the cost of merchandise and collected at the place of sale.

Go Figure

Name_____ Period_____ Date_____

Think Read and analyze.

The sum of the measurements of the angles of a triangle is 180°. Find the missing angle measurement for each triangle.

1.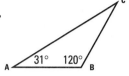

2.

3.

4.

_____

5.

6.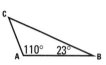

7.

8.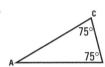

_____

Solve Show and label your work here.

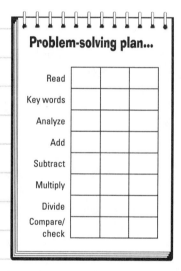

Problem-solving plan...

Read			
Key words			
Analyze			
Add			
Subtract			
Multiply			
Divide			
Compare/ check			

Communicate Explain the strategies and thinking processes used to solve the problem(s).

Vocabulary

sum—The answer to an addition problem.

angle—A shape formed by two rays with a common point of origin called a vertex.

triangle—A two-dimensional closed figure that has three sides and three angles.

Go Figure

Name_____ Period_____ Date_____

Think   Read and analyze.

Rodney wanted to know how many times the digit 5 showed up in the numbers from 1 to 100.

A. Create a representation to solve the problem.

B. How many 5s did he find? _____

Solve   Show and label your work here.

Communicate   Explain the strategies and thinking processes used to solve the problem(s).

Vocabulary

digit—Any single whole number 0 through 9.

representation—A picture that shows a mathematical idea or relationship.

Try This!

Go Figure

Name_____ Period_____ Date_____

Think — Read and analyze.

Wholesalers provide goods to stores for less than the retail price. The difference between the wholesale price and the retail price is the profit a merchant makes for selling a product. If Joe's Deli buys 100 boxes of hot dogs at $5.75 a box, how many boxes of hot dogs will Joe have to sell at $25.75 to make a profit of $400?

_____

Problem-solving plan...

Read			
Key words			
Analyze			
Add			
Subtract			
Multiply			
Divide			
Compare/ check			

Solve — Show and label your work here.

_____
_____
_____
_____
_____
_____
_____
_____

Communicate — Explain the strategies and thinking processes used to solve the problem(s).

_____
_____
_____
_____
_____
_____

Vocabulary

This section may be used to introduce or reinforce any mathematical words or phrases.

_____
_____
_____
_____
_____
_____

Go Figure

Name_____ Period_____ Date_____

Think — Read and analyze.

Moshie claims he has a better job than Tyra. He makes $60.00 for 8 hours of work at the local sporting goods store. Tyra works 6 hours and makes $49.50 at the supermarket. Who makes more money per hour and what is the difference?

_____

Problem-solving plan...

Read			
Key words			
Analyze			
Add			
Subtract			
Multiply			
Divide			
Compare/ check			

Solve — Show and label your work here.

Communicate — Explain the strategies and thinking processes used to solve the problem(s).

Vocabulary

difference—The answer to a subtraction problem.

Go Figure

Name_____ Period_____ Date_____

Think Read and analyze.

Compute the perimeter of the polygons and the circumference of the circles.

Formulas: Perimeter of a triangle: $P = s + s + s$

Perimeter of a rectangle: $P = 2l + 2w$

Circumference of a circle: $C = 2\pi r$ or πd. Use 3.14 for π.

Problem-solving plan...

Read			
Key words			
Analyze			
Add			
Subtract			
Multiply			
Divide			
Compare/ check			

1.
$20\frac{2}{5}''$
$15\frac{1}{5}''$
$13''$

2.
4.1 in.
5.2 in.

3.
15 ft
$12\frac{1}{3}$ ft

4.
41 cm

5.
28 cm
34 cm

6.
40 cm

_____ _____ _____

Solve Show and label your work here.

Communicate Explain the strategies and thinking processes used to solve the problem(s).

Vocabulary

perimeter—The distance around the outside of a two-dimensional shape.

polygon—A two-dimensional closed shape with three or more straight lines.

circumference—The distance around a circle.

circle—A closed curved shape that has all points an equal distance from the center.

triangle—A two-dimensional figure that has three sides and three angles.

rectangle—A parallelogram with four right angles.

pi (π)—The ratio of the circumference of a circle to its diameter ($\pi \approx 3.14$ or $\frac{22}{7}$).

Go Figure

Name_____ Period_____ Date_____

Read and analyze.

A. Fill in the blanks with **mean**, **median**, and **mode**.

1. The _____ is the middle value in a distribution, above and below which lie an equal number of values.

2. The_____ is the arithmetic average for a set of data.

3. The _____ is the number item that occurs most often in a set of data.

B. Find the mean, median, and mode for this set of data.

14, 6, 3, 8, 20, 20, 3, 7, 30, 3, 15, 25

mean = _____   median = _____   mode = _____

Problem-solving plan...

Read			
Key words			
Analyze			
Add			
Subtract			
Multiply			
Divide			
Compare/ check			

Solve Show and label your work here.

Communicate Explain the strategies and thinking processes used to solve the problem(s).

Vocabulary

set—A grouping of similar things.

mean—The sum of a set of data divided by the number of items in the set.

median—The middle value in a distribution, above and below which lie an equal number of values.

mode—The data item that occurs most often in a set of data.

22

Name_____ Period_____ Date_____

Simone said that a **prime number** is a positive number greater than 1 that has only two factors: itself and 1. For example, 3 is a prime number because the only way to multiply and get 3 is 1 × 3.

When Jake did his homework, he found 15 prime numbers between 1 and 50. What numbers did Jake find?

_____

Problem-solving plan...

Read			
Key words			
Analyze			
Add			
Subtract			
Multiply			
Divide			
Compare/ check			

Solve **Show and label your work here.**

Communicate Explain the strategies and thinking processes used to solve the problem(s).

Vocabulary

prime number—A positive whole number greater than 1 that has only two factors, itself and 1.

factor—A number that divides evenly into another number, leaving no remainder.

Go Figure

Name_____ Period_____ Date_____

Think and Solve   Read and analyze.

A. Identify these acute, right, and obtuse angles.

1.

2.

3.

4.

89° = _____

_____   _____   _____

5.

6.

132° = _____

7.

90° = _____

8.

_____   _____   _____   _____

9.

50° = _____

10.

11.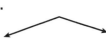

12.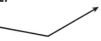

_____   _____   _____

13.

75° = _____

14.

15.

10° = _____

16.

169° = _____

_____

B. Draw, label, and define an obtuse, acute, and right angle.

1.   2.   3.

_____   _____   _____

_____   _____   _____

_____   _____   _____

Communicate   Explain the strategies and thinking processes used to solve the problem(s).

_____

_____

_____

_____

_____

_____

Vocabulary

This section may be used to introduce or reinforce any mathematical words or phrases.

_____

_____

_____

_____

_____

_____

Try This!　　　　　　　　　　　　　　　　　　**Go Figure**

Name_____ Period_____ Date_____

Think　Read and analyze.

A. Find the mean, median, and mode for this set of data.

16, 22, 8, 13, 19, 28, 13

Mean: _____ Median: _____ Mode: _____

B. Find the mean, median, and mode for this set of data.

98, 62, 75, 42, 78, 62, 71, 62

Mean: _____ Median: _____ Mode: _____

C. Which of the three types of averages—mean, median, or mode—is the most useful to a shoe manufacturer in projecting the number of each size of shoe to produce?

_____

_____

Problem-solving plan...

Read			
Key words			
Analyze			
Add			
Subtract			
Multiply			
Divide			
Compare/ check			

Solve　Show and label your work here.

Communicate　Explain the strategies and thinking processes used to solve the problem(s).

Vocabulary

This section may be used to introduce or reinforce any mathematical words or phrases.

_____

_____

_____

_____

_____

_____

Go Figure

Name_____ Period_____ Date_____

Think — Read and analyze.

A bag contains 2 green, 5 yellow, 6 red, and 3 pink buttons. If Zulika reaches into the bag without looking, what is the probability that she will pick a red button?

$$\text{Probability (Event)} = \frac{\text{number of favorable outcomes}}{\text{total number of possible outcomes}}$$

_____

Problem-solving plan...

Read			
Key words			
Analyze			
Add			
Subtract			
Multiply			
Divide			
Compare/ check			

Solve — Show and label your work here.

_____
_____
_____
_____
_____
_____
_____
_____
_____

Communicate — Explain the strategies and thinking processes used to solve the problem(s).

_____
_____
_____
_____
_____
_____
_____

Vocabulary

probability—The likelihood that a specific event or set of outcomes will occur. It can be expressed as a ratio, fraction, decimal, or percent.

Go Figure

Name_____ Period_____ Date_____

Carlos drew a geometric figure using ordered pairs.

A. On the grid below, graph the points for the following ordered pairs and connect them to make a single closed figure.

(5, 9), (10, 4), (10, 7), (3, 4), (8, 9), (5, 2), (3, 7), and (8, 2)

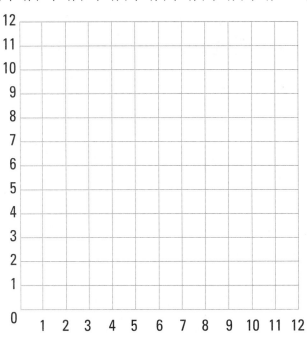

B. Give two correct names for this figure: _____

C. Using three of the graphed points, make a right triangle.

D. Using four of the graphed points, make a trapezoid.

_____

_____

_____

_____

_____

_____

_____

_____

Vocabulary

ordered pair—A pair of numbers (x, y) that describes the location of a point on a grid.

grid—A framework of horizontal and vertical lines that forms squares for graphing information.

graph (v)—To make a visual representation of information or data.

right triangle—A triangle with one right angle (90°).

trapezoid—A four-sided closed figure with only one set of parallel lines.

Go Figure

Name_____ Period_____ Date_____

Think — Read and analyze.

A. Three teenagers start a Home Helper business the summer before college. They charge each homeowner a flat rate of $325. For this flat rate, they mow lawns, water plants, feed and walk pets, and do other odd jobs by appointment. If they work for 4 months and their expenses are $225 per month, how many homeowners must sign up for their service for each teenager to earn $1,500? _____

B. Underline any information in the problem that does not contribute to the solution.

Problem-solving plan...

Read			
Key words			
Analyze			
Add			
Subtract			
Multiply			
Divide			
Compare/ check			

Solve — Show and label your work here.

Communicate — Explain the strategies and thinking processes used to solve the problem(s).

Vocabulary

flat rate—One single amount of money charged for a combination of services.

Go Figure

Name_____ Period_____ Date_____

Read and analyze.

A. Using the following descriptions, label and draw the geometric figures.

_____

1. An angle that is less than 90°

   _____

   _____

_____

2. A two-dimensional figure with four congruent sides

   _____

   _____

_____

3. An angle that measures more than 90° but less than 180°

   _____

   _____

_____

4. An angle of less than 90° that has been divided into two equal parts

   _____

   _____

5. A triangle that has three congruent sides

   _____

   _____

_____

6. A two-dimensional four-sided figure that has four right angles

   _____

   _____

_____

B. Which of the above figures are parallelograms? Why? _____

_____

_____

Explain the strategies and thinking processes used to solve the problem(s).

_____

_____

_____

_____

_____

_____

Vocabulary

parallelogram—A four-sided, two-dimensional figure that has parallel opposite sides.

congruent—In geometric figures, having the same measurement.

Go Figure

Name_____ Period_____ Date_____

Think   Read and analyze.

Reina went to the clothing store with a $50 bill. She wanted to buy a sweater for $8.79, a skirt for $11.50, 2 pairs of earrings for $5.40 a pair, and a jacket for $21.29. Is her $50 bill enough to pay for these purchases? If it is, how much will she have left over? If not, how much more money would she need?

_____

Problem-solving plan...

Read			
Key words			
Analyze			
Add			
Subtract			
Multiply			
Divide			
Compare/ check			

Solve   Show and label your work here.

Communicate   Explain the strategies and thinking processes used to solve the problem(s).

Vocabulary

This section may be used to introduce or reinforce any mathematical words or phrases.

_____

_____

_____

_____

_____

_____

Try This!

Name_____ Period_____ Date_____

Go Figure

Think   Read and analyze.

Dominic put 3 pennies, 6 nickels, 7 dimes, and 4 quarters in a can.
He casually reached into the can and randomly selected a coin.
What is the probability that he selected a dime?

_____

Problem-solving plan...

Read			
Key words			
Analyze			
Add			
Subtract			
Multiply			
Divide			
Compare/ check			

Solve   Show and label your work here.

Communicate   Explain the strategies and thinking processes used to solve the problem(s).

Vocabulary

This section may be used to introduce or reinforce any mathematical words or phrases.

_____

_____

_____

_____

_____

_____

Go Figure

Name_____ Period_____ Date_____

Think — Read and analyze.

Big bargains can be found at the Discount Computer Store. You can buy an 80-gigabyte computer for $795, a 17-inch flat monitor for $329, and an 832C printer for $175. Wanda's Computer Shop is charging $1,488 for the same equipment.

A. Estimate which store has the better deal. _____ has the better deal. The estimated price is _____.

B. What is the price at the Discount Computer Store? _____

C. How much would you save by buying the equipment at the Discount Computer Store? _____

Problem-solving plan...

Read			
Key words			
Analyze			
Add			
Subtract			
Multiply			
Divide			
Compare/ check			

Solve — Show and label your work here.

Communicate — Explain the strategies and thinking processes used to solve the problem(s).

Vocabulary

discount—An amount of money subtracted from a selling price.

estimate—To make an educated guess based on information in the problem; often involves rounding.

Go Figure

Think Read and analyze.

A. On a winter morning, the temperature was –8° Fahrenheit (F). By 3:00 P.M., the temperature had risen 21° F. What was the temperature at 3:00 P.M.? _____

B. Later in the week, the temperature reached a high of 8° F before dropping 25° F to the day's low. What was the low temperature for that day? _____

C. Represent the solutions using number lines. Show the tick marks.

Problem-solving plan...

Read			
Key words			
Analyze			
Add			
Subtract			
Multiply			
Divide			
Compare/ check			

Solve Show and label your work here.

Communicate Explain the strategies and thinking processes used to solve the problem(s).

Vocabulary

Fahrenheit—A temperature scale that registers the freezing point of water at 32° F and the boiling point of water at 212° F.

number line—A line with equally spaced points that represent numbers.

tick marks—The points on a number line.

Go Figure

Name_____ Period_____ Date_____

Think   Read and analyze.

A. The pet store had 15 puppies for sale. Nine of the puppies were beagles. What percent of the puppies were beagles? _____

B. What percent of the large square is shaded? _____

Problem-solving plan...

Read			
Key words			
Analyze			
Add			
Subtract			
Multiply			
Divide			
Compare/ check			

Solve   Show and label your work here.

Communicate   Explain the strategies and thinking processes used to solve the problem(s).

Vocabulary

percent—One part of a whole that has been divided into 100 equal parts.

Name_____ Period_____ Date_____

Think and Solve **Read and analyze.**

A. Identify and label the parallel, perpendicular, and intersecting lines.

1.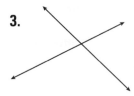

2.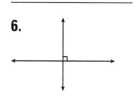

3.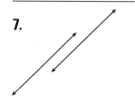

4.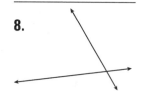

_____

5.

6.

7.

8.

_____

In the illustration on the right,

9. $\overleftrightarrow{CD}$ and $\overleftrightarrow{AB}$ are _____.

10. $\overleftrightarrow{CD}$ and $\overleftrightarrow{GH}$ are _____.

11. $\overleftrightarrow{AB}$ and $\overleftrightarrow{EF}$ are _____.

12. $\overleftrightarrow{EF}$ and $\overleftrightarrow{GH}$ are _____.

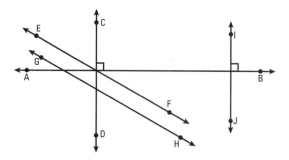

B. On a separate sheet of paper, draw a figure similar to the one used for the four questions above. Write four questions about your figure and give the correct answers.

Communicate **Explain the strategies and thinking processes used to solve the problem(s).**

_____

_____

_____

_____

_____

_____

_____

Vocabulary

line—A line is straight, has no thickness, and continues in both directions without end.

parallel lines—Lines that lie in the same plane and never intersect.

perpendicular lines—Lines that lie in the same plane and intersect at a right (90°) angle.

intersecting lines—Lines that lie in the same plane and cross each other, forming vertical and adjacent angles.

Go Figure

35

Name_____ Period_____ Date_____

Think   Read and analyze.

This is a permutation problem.

A. Roy has 5 pairs of pants and 8 shirts. How many different combinations can he make with these articles of clothing? _____

B. Draw a representation to show the solution to this question.

Problem-solving plan...

Read			
Key words			
Analyze			
Add			
Subtract			
Multiply			
Divide			
Compare/ check			

Solve   Show and label your work here.

Communicate   Explain the strategies and thinking processes used to solve the problem(s).

Vocabulary

permutation—An ordered arrangement (combination) of all or some of the items of a set.

combination—The result of putting two or more things together.

representation—A picture that shows a mathematical idea or relationship.

35

Try This!

Go Figure

Name_____ Period_____ Date_____

Think Read and analyze.

A. There are 35 members in the Chess Club. Fourteen of the members are female. What percent of the club is male?

_____

B. Make a geometric figure that shades 28% of this graph paper.

Problem-solving plan...

Read			
Key words			
Analyze			
Add			
Subtract			
Multiply			
Divide			
Compare/ check			

Solve Show and label your work here.

Communicate Explain the strategies and thinking processes used to solve the problem(s).

Vocabulary

This section may be used to introduce or reinforce any mathematical words or phrases.

_____

_____

_____

_____

_____

Go Figure

Name_____ Period_____ Date_____

Think   **Read and analyze.**

Laura completely filled the empty gas tank of her car before starting her trip. The tank held 21 gallons and she paid $1.499 per gallon. After driving 360 miles to her destination, she again filled the tank. This time she added 18 gallons at $1.439 per gallon.

A. How many miles per gallon does her car get? _____

B. What was the total cost of gasoline for the first leg of her trip? _____

C. If Laura's return trip took 18 gallons of gas that cost $1.439 a gallon, what was the total cost of gasoline for her trip? _____

Problem-solving plan...

Read			
Key words			
Analyze			
Add			
Subtract			
Multiply			
Divide			
Compare/check			

Solve   **Show and label your work here.**

Communicate   **Explain the strategies and thinking processes used to solve the problem(s).**

Vocabulary

This section may be used to introduce or reinforce any mathematical words or phrases.

_____

_____

_____

_____

_____

_____

Go Figure

Name_____ Period_____ Date_____

Think Read and analyze.

Paulette is putting a wallpaper border around her bedroom 3 feet up from the floor. The dimensions of her bedroom are shown below. The drawing shows that she needs to plan for two windows and a doorway.

```
 window        window
 2.5 ft        2.5 ft


                      10 ft



       doorway
       3 ft
  ——— 12 ft ———
```

A. How many feet of border does she need to purchase?

_____

B. The border costs $16 per 5-yard roll. How much will it cost to paper her room? _____

Problem-solving plan...

Read			
Key words			
Analyze			
Add			
Subtract			
Multiply			
Divide			
Compare/check			

Solve Show and label your work here.

Communicate Explain the strategies and thinking processes used to solve the problem(s).

Vocabulary

dimension—Measurement of spatial proportions such as width, height, and length.

Go Figure

Name_____ Period_____ Date_____

Think — Read and analyze.

Three students in Ms. Toad's biology class were comparing their test scores. The scores were represented as fractions. Timothy answered $\frac{4}{5}$ of the questions correctly, Terri answered $\frac{2}{6}$ correctly, and Wanda answered $\frac{9}{10}$ correctly. Put their scores in order from highest to lowest.

_____

Problem-solving plan...

Read			
Key words			
Analyze			
Add			
Subtract			
Multiply			
Divide			
Compare/ check			

Solve — Show and label your work here.

Communicate — Explain the strategies and thinking processes used to solve the problem(s).

Vocabulary

fraction—A part of one whole unit. ($\frac{1}{2}$ = 1 of 2 equal parts; $\frac{3}{4}$ = 3 of 4 equal parts.)

Name_____ Period_____ Date_____

Think and Solve Read and analyze.

A. Identify and label the parallel, perpendicular, and intersecting lines.

1.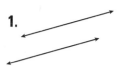

_____

2.

_____

3.

_____

4.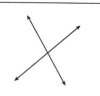

_____

5.

_____

6.

_____

7.

_____

8.

_____

In the illustration on the right,

9. $\overleftrightarrow{AB}$ and $\overleftrightarrow{CD}$ are _____.

10. $\overleftrightarrow{CD}$ and $\overleftrightarrow{FG}$ are _____.

11. $\overleftrightarrow{HI}$ and $\overleftrightarrow{FG}$ are _____.

12. $\overleftrightarrow{FG}$ and $\overleftrightarrow{EZ}$ are _____.

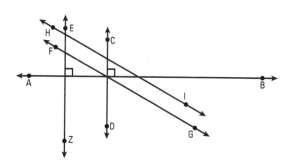

B. Draw and label perpendicular, parallel, and intersecting lines.

1.   **2.**   **3.**

_____   _____   _____

Communicate Explain the strategies and thinking processes used to solve the problem(s).

_____

_____

_____

_____

_____

_____

Vocabulary

line—A line is straight, has no thickness, and continues in both directions without end.

parallel lines—Lines that lie in the same plane and never intersect.

perpendicular lines—Lines that lie in the same plane and intersect at a right (90°) angle.

intersecting lines—Lines that lie in the same plane and cross each other, forming vertical and adjacent angles.

Go Figure

Name_____ Period_____ Date_____

Think and Solve   Read and analyze.

An ordered pair is a pair of numbers that describe the location of a point on a coordinate plane. Ordered pairs are in the form (x, y).

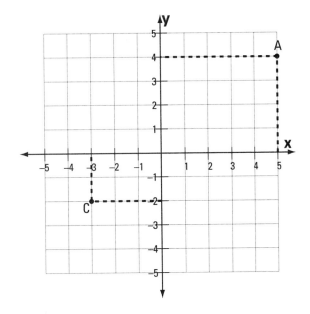

Problem-solving plan...

Read			
Key words			
Analyze			
Add			
Subtract			
Multiply			
Divide			
Compare/ check			

1. Point A is located at _____

2. Point C is located at _____

3. Graph the point P (4, 2).

4. Graph the point Z (−5, −2).

5. Graph the point H (−4, 3).

Communicate   Explain the strategies and thinking processes used to solve the problem(s).

_____

_____

_____

_____

_____

_____

_____

_____

Vocabulary

ordered pair—A pair of numbers (x, y) that describes the location of a point on a coordinate plane.

coordinate plane—A set of perpendicular number lines that intersect at their zero points (the point of origin). The horizontal line is called the x-axis and the vertical line is called the y-axis.

Try This!

Go Figure

Name_____ Period_____ Date_____

Think **Read and analyze.**

Kawana is planning to put a railing around his patio. The patio is on two levels. He will put the railing around the upper level from the house to where the lower level begins and around the outside of the lower level. He will not need railing where the upper level leads to the lower level.

A. Calculate the missing measurements and determine how many feet of railing Kawana needs. _____

B. What will Kawana's cost be if the railing comes in 3' lengths at $22 per length? _____

[figure: patio diagram with labels: 7', 4', upper level, house, 9', 18', 6', 3', lower level]

Solve **Show and label your work here.**

_____
_____
_____
_____
_____
_____
_____
_____

Problem-solving plan...

Read			
Key words			
Analyze			
Add			
Subtract			
Multiply			
Divide			
Compare/ check			

Communicate **Explain the strategies and thinking processes used to solve the problem(s).**

_____
_____
_____
_____
_____

Vocabulary

This section may be used to introduce or reinforce any mathematical words or phrases.

_____
_____
_____
_____
_____
_____

Go Figure

Name_____ Period_____ Date_____

● ●

Think   Read and analyze.

Sarah is a competitive swimmer, and she swims every day. On Monday, she swam 5.0 miles; on Tuesday and Wednesday, she swam 6.5 miles each day; on Thursday, she swam 4.8 miles; and on Friday, she swam 7.2 miles.

A. What is the average number of miles Sarah swam each day during the week? _____

B. What is the average number of feet Sarah swam each day? _____ (One mile equals 5,280 feet.)

C. If Sarah averaged 7.4 miles per day the next week, how many more feet did she swim each day on average that week? _____

Problem-solving plan...

Read			
Key words			
Analyze			
Add			
Subtract			
Multiply			
Divide			
Compare/ check			

Solve   Show and label your work here.

_____

_____

_____

_____

_____

_____

_____

_____

_____

_____

Communicate   Explain the strategies and thinking processes used to solve the problem(s).

_____

_____

_____

_____

_____

_____

Vocabulary

average—The sum of the values of a set of items divided by the number of items.

Go Figure

Name_____ Period_____ Date_____

Think   Read and analyze.

Toliver tried to stump his sister Myrta with a math problem. He said, "I'm thinking of two consecutive numbers whose product is 72 and whose sum is 17. What are the two numbers?"

Myrta thought for a minute and said, "The numbers are _____ and _____." Check the answer.

Problem-solving plan...

Read			
Key words			
Analyze			
Add			
Subtract			
Multiply			
Divide			
Compare/ check			

Solve   Show and label your work here.

Communicate   Explain the strategies and thinking processes used to solve the problem(s).

Vocabulary

consecutive numbers— Numbers that follow each other in a sequential pattern. (Example: 1, 2, 3— consecutive numbers; 2, 4, 6—consecutive even numbers; 1, 3, 5—consecutive odd numbers)

product—The answer to a multiplication problem.

sum—The answer to an addition problem.

Go Figure

Name_____ Period_____ Date_____

Think — Read and analyze.

A. On the lines provided in **Solve**, write the given integers in sequence from least to greatest.

4,857	−3,253	5,858	−8,565	−4,849
6,549	−7,948	−5,483	−2,094	0

B. Circle the integers that have 5 in the hundreds place.

C. Underline the integers that have 5 in the tens place.

Problem-solving plan...

Read			
Key words			
Analyze			
Add			
Subtract			
Multiply			
Divide			
Compare/ check			

Solve — Show and label your work here.

_____

_____

Communicate — Explain the strategies and thinking processes used to solve the problem(s).

Vocabulary

integer—One of the set of whole numbers, their opposites, and 0 (... −2, −1, 0, 1, 2...).

sequence—The order in which a set of items is arranged.

hundreds place—The third digit to the left in a whole number or the third digit to the left of a decimal point.

tens place—The second digit to the left in a whole number or the second digit to the left of a decimal point.

Go Figure

Name_____ Period_____ Date_____

Think **Read and analyze.**

Larry W. McCoy bought a computer game at Computer Games, Inc. The price for the computer game was $17. This price was 20% off the original price. There was a further discount of 15% off the ticketed price.

A. What was the original price of the computer game? _____

B. What was the final price of the computer game? _____

C. Complete the blank check to show how Larry paid for the game.

Problem-solving plan...

Read			
Key words			
Analyze			
Add			
Subtract			
Multiply			
Divide			
Compare/ check			

Solve **Show and label your work here.**

Larry W. McCoy
670 Eastman St.
Denver, CO 80239

0735

Date _____

Pay to the order of _____ $ [____]

_____ Dollars

State Bank & Trust
169 Bugle Street
Denver, CO 80249

⑆ 2035960891 000027849611 0735

Communicate **Explain the strategies and thinking processes used to solve the problem(s).**

Vocabulary

discount—An amount of money subtracted from a selling price.

check (*n*)—A written order to a bank to pay the amount specified from funds on deposit.

Go Figure

Name_____ Period_____ Date_____

Think — Read and analyze.

Edgar is going to fence his vegetable garden. The dimensions of the garden are shown below.

20 ft [rectangle]

75 ft

A. How many feet of fence are needed to completely surround the garden?

_____

B. How many square feet does Edgar have for planting vegetables?

_____

Problem-solving plan...

Read			
Key words			
Analyze			
Add			
Subtract			
Multiply			
Divide			
Compare/ check			

Solve — Show and label your work here.

_____

_____

_____

_____

_____

_____

_____

_____

_____

Communicate — Explain the strategies and thinking processes used to solve the problem(s).

_____

_____

_____

_____

_____

_____

_____

Vocabulary

dimension—A measurement, especially width, height, or length.

Try This!   **Go Figure**

Name_____ Period_____ Date_____

Think   Read and analyze.

What are two consecutive numbers whose sum is 15 and whose product is 56? Check your answer.

_____

Problem-solving plan...

Read			
Key words			
Analyze			
Add			
Subtract			
Multiply			
Divide			
Compare/ check			

Solve   Show and label your work here.

Communicate   Explain the strategies and thinking processes used to solve the problem(s).

Vocabulary

This section may be used to introduce or reinforce any mathematical words or phrases.

_____

_____

_____

_____

_____

Go Figure

Name_____ Period_____ Date_____

Think   **Read and analyze.**

A. Jamaar's father agreed to help Jamaar buy a new car. His father agreed to pay 40 percent of the price of a car if Jamaar would pay the rest. They found a car for $4,200. How much did each pay?

_____

B. For his portion of the cost, Jamaar obtained a loan from his grandmother at 6 percent interest. He is paying off the loan in 36 equal monthly installments. How much does he pay each month? _____

Problem-solving plan...

Read			
Key words			
Analyze			
Add			
Subtract			
Multiply			
Divide			
Compare/ check			

Solve   **Show and label your work here.**

Communicate   **Explain the strategies and thinking processes used to solve the problem(s).**

Vocabulary

percent—One part of a whole that has been divided into 100 equal parts.

loan—An amount of money borrowed (usually for interest) that must be paid back.

interest—The amount paid for the use of money.

installments—Successive payments to pay off a debt.

Go Figure

Name_____ Period_____ Date_____

Think Read and analyze.

This is a logic problem.

There are five children in the Stewart family—Carl, Donna, Allen, Beth, and Gary. Most of them are fussy about the vegetables they eat.

A. Construct a table for the following information.

Donna and Allen eat broccoli.
Carl, Donna, and Gary eat corn, peas, and spinach.
Beth and Donna eat potatoes, and Beth also eats corn.

B. Which child would probably grumble least at the dinner table?

_____

C. What is the favorite vegetable in the Stewart family? _____

D. Who doesn't like potatoes but likes broccoli? _____

Problem-solving plan...			
Read			
Key words			
Analyze			
Add			
Subtract			
Multiply			
Divide			
Compare/ check			

Solve Show and label your work here.

Communicate Explain the strategies and thinking processes used to solve the problem(s).

_____
_____
_____
_____
_____
_____
_____

Vocabulary

logic—The science of sound thinking and proof by reasoning.

table—An arrangement of data for easy reference.

Go Figure

Name_____ Period_____ Date_____

Think   Read and analyze.

Compute the area of the rectangles, triangles, and circles.

Formulas: Area of a rectangle: A = lw

Area of a triangle: $A = \frac{1}{2}bh$

Area of a circle: $A = \pi r^2$. Use 3.14 for π.

Problem-solving plan...			
Read			
Key words			
Analyze			
Add			
Subtract			
Multiply			
Divide			
Compare/ check			

1.
21 in.
13 in.

2.
9 in.
3.5 in.

3.
5 in.
6 in.

_____   _____   _____

4.
15 cm
13 cm

5.
9 in.

6.
31 in.
14 in.

_____   _____   _____

Solve   Show and label your work here.

_____
_____
_____
_____
_____
_____
_____

Communicate   Explain the strategies and thinking processes used to solve the problem(s).

_____
_____
_____
_____
_____
_____

Vocabulary

area—The surface inside a closed two-dimensional figure or region.

rectangle—A parallelogram with four right angles.

triangle—A two-dimensional closed figure that has three sides and three angles.

circle—A closed curved shape that has all points an equal distance from the center.

formula—A recipe or equation used to solve a mathematical problem.

pi (π)—The ratio of the circumference of a circle to its diameter ($\pi \approx 3.14$ or $\frac{22}{7}$).

Go Figure

Name_____ Period_____ Date_____

Think — Read and analyze.

Kalina has been saving her pocket change in a jar. Her jar contains 35 pennies, 25 nickels, 8 dimes, and 17 quarters. She takes one coin out of the jar without looking. In terms of percent, what is the probability that she gets a quarter? _____

Problem-solving plan...

Read			
Key words			
Analyze			
Add			
Subtract			
Multiply			
Divide			
Compare/ check			

Solve — Show and label your work here.

Communicate — Explain the strategies and thinking processes used to solve the problem(s).

Vocabulary

percent—One part of a whole that has been divided into 100 equal parts.

probability—The likelihood that a specific event or set of outcomes will occur. It can be expressed as a ratio, fraction, decimal, or percent.

Go Figure

Name_____ Period_____ Date_____

Think Read and analyze.

Tai opened his social studies book randomly. Looking at the page numbers, he found that the sum of the numbers of the two facing pages was 849. To which pages did he open the book? _____

Problem-solving plan...

Read			
Key words			
Analyze			
Add			
Subtract			
Multiply			
Divide			
Compare/ check			

Solve Show and label your work here.

Communicate Explain the strategies and thinking processes used to solve the problem(s).

Vocabulary

random—Having no predetermined pattern or plan; by chance.

sum—The answer to an addition problem.

Try This!

Go Figure

Name_____ Period_____ Date_____

Read and analyze.

Mr. Tucker had five customers come into his pet store to buy puppies. Each of the customers had likes and dislikes about puppies.

A. Construct a table for the following information:

Fred and Wanda like poodles.

Cedric, Fred, and Tye like beagles, cocker spaniels, and golden retrievers.

Sam and Fred like terriers, and Sam also likes beagles.

B. Which customer would be pleased to have any one of the puppies? _____

C. Which puppy is the favorite? _____

D. Who doesn't like terriers but likes poodles? _____

Solve **Show and label your work here.**

_____
_____
_____
_____
_____
_____
_____
_____
_____
_____

Communicate **Explain the strategies and thinking processes used to solve the problem(s).**

_____
_____
_____
_____
_____

Vocabulary

This section may be used to introduce or reinforce any mathematical words or phrases.

_____
_____
_____
_____
_____
_____

Go Figure

Name_____ Period_____ Date_____

Think   Read and analyze.

A. *Brink's Book of Events* records the highest number of sit-ups done at one time as 4,500. The sit-ups were completed in 3 hours and 52 minutes. Calvin can do 23 sit-ups in a minute. How many minutes would it take him to tie the record? _____

B. Express the above answer in hours and minutes. Round your answer to the nearest minute. _____

Problem-solving plan...

Read			
Key words			
Analyze			
Add			
Subtract			
Multiply			
Divide			
Compare/ check			

Solve   Show and label your work here.

Communicate   Explain the strategies and thinking processes used to solve the problem(s).

Vocabulary

This section may be used to introduce or reinforce any mathematical words or phrases.

_____
_____
_____
_____
_____
_____

Go Figure

Name_____ Period_____ Date_____

Think and Solve Read and analyze.

A. Research the following shapes to identify and name the following figures.

1. _____

2. _____

3. _____

4. _____

5. _____

6. _____

7. _____

8. _____

9. _____

10. _____

11. _____

12. _____

B. Draw and define the following figures.

1. trapezoid _____

2. polygon _____

Communicate Explain the strategies and thinking processes used to solve the problem(s).

_____

Vocabulary

This section may be used to introduce or reinforce any mathematical words or phrases.

_____

Go Figure

Name_____ Period_____ Date_____

Think Read and analyze.

In 1997, Devon bought a house for $150,000. His real estate agent predicted that the house would increase in value about $9,500 every year. In 2002, Devon sold the house for $207,000.

A. Was the real estate agent's prediction correct? _____

B. What was the difference between the predicted increase in value and the actual increase in value? _____

C. Was this to Devon's advantage or disadvantage? Explain.

_____

_____

_____

Problem-solving plan...

Read			
Key words			
Analyze			
Add			
Subtract			
Multiply			
Divide			
Compare/ check			

Solve Show and label your work here.

Communicate Explain the strategies and thinking processes used to solve the problem(s).

Vocabulary

predict—To make an educated guess about a future event.

Go Figure

Name_____ Period_____ Date_____

Think Read and analyze.

The weights of the players of the high school football team are as follows:

189, 157, 142, 167, 149, 178, 153, 185, 148, 192, 164, 172

Find the mean, median, and mode for this set of data.

Mean: _____   Median: _____   Mode: _____

Problem-solving plan...

Read			
Key words			
Analyze			
Add			
Subtract			
Multiply			
Divide			
Compare/ check			

Solve Show and label your work here.

Communicate Explain the strategies and thinking processes used to solve the problem(s).

Vocabulary

mean—The arithmetic average; the values of the items in a set of data divided by the number of items.

median—The middle value in a set of data, above and below which lie an equal number of values.

mode—The value that occurs most often in a set of data.

Go Figure

Name_____ Period_____ Date_____

Read and analyze.

In preparing for the board of directors meeting, the planners decided to give each of the 35 board members a folder containing the following materials: 3 pencils, 5 pens, 6 writing pads (each containing 20 sheets of paper), and 11 company logos.

A. How many pencils will the planners need? _____

B. How many sheets of writing paper are there altogether? _____

C. How many company logos will they need? _____

D. How many pens will they need? _____

E. How many folders will they need? _____

Problem-solving plan...

Read			
Key words			
Analyze			
Add			
Subtract			
Multiply			
Divide			
Compare/check			

Solve **Show and label your work here.**

_____
_____
_____
_____
_____
_____
_____
_____
_____
_____
_____
_____

Communicate Explain the strategies and thinking processes used to solve the problem(s).

_____
_____
_____
_____
_____
_____
_____

Vocabulary

This section may be used to introduce or reinforce any mathematical words or phrases.

_____
_____
_____
_____
_____
_____

Try This!

Go Figure

Name_____ Period_____ Date_____

Read and analyze.

Omar wanted to buy a car that would hold its value. The *Car Buyer's Report* said that the car he bought would decrease in value approximately $300 a year, depending on use. Omar bought the car for $4,000 and sold it 3 years later for $2,500.

Problem-solving plan...

Read			
Key words			
Analyze			
Add			
Subtract			
Multiply			
Divide			
Compare/ check			

A. What is the difference between the predicted resale price and the actual resale price of Omar's car? _____

B. Is this difference to Omar's advantage or disadvantage? Explain. _____
_____
_____

C. What might be some of the reasons for this difference? _____
_____
_____

Solve   **Show and label your work here.**

_____
_____
_____
_____
_____
_____

Communicate   **Explain the strategies and thinking processes used to solve the problem(s).**

_____
_____
_____
_____
_____
_____
_____

Vocabulary

This section may be used to introduce or reinforce any mathematical words or phrases.

_____
_____
_____
_____
_____
_____

Go Figure

Name_____ Period_____ Date_____

Think   Read and analyze.

Tara bought a new pair of skis on sale. The skis had originally been priced at $280.00 but had been successively discounted 25% and 30%. What did Tara pay for the skis? _____

Problem-solving plan...

Read			
Key words			
Analyze			
Add			
Subtract			
Multiply			
Divide			
Compare/check			

Solve   Show and label your work here.

Communicate   Explain the strategies and thinking processes used to solve the problem(s).

Vocabulary

discount—An amount of money subtracted from a selling price.

Go Figure

Name_____ Period_____ Date_____

Think   Read and analyze.

To convert a fraction to a decimal, divide the numerator by the denominator. Put a decimal point after the numerator and add two or three zeros to carry the answer out two or three decimal places.

Example:
$$\frac{4}{5} = 5\overline{)4.00} = 0.80$$

A.
1. $\frac{7}{8}$ = _____
2. $\frac{2}{5}$ = _____
3. $\frac{1}{4}$ = _____
4. $\frac{2}{3}$ = _____

5. $\frac{1}{2}$ = _____
6. $\frac{4}{5}$ = _____
7. $\frac{1}{3}$ = _____
8. $\frac{1}{5}$ = _____

9. $\frac{1}{8}$ = _____
10. $\frac{3}{4}$ = _____
11. $\frac{3}{5}$ = _____
12. $\frac{5}{8}$ = _____

13. $\frac{3}{8}$ = _____
14. $\frac{7}{10}$ = _____
15. $\frac{17}{25}$ = _____
16. $\frac{19}{20}$ = _____

B. Jenny ate $\frac{2}{5}$ of a pizza. Freddie ate $\frac{1}{4}$ of the pizza. What percent of the pizza did they eat? _____

C. What percent of the pizza was left? _____

Solve   Show and label your work here.

_____
_____
_____
_____
_____
_____
_____
_____
_____
_____
_____

Communicate   Explain the strategies and thinking processes used to solve the problem(s).

_____
_____
_____
_____

Vocabulary

fraction—A part of one whole unit. ($\frac{1}{2}$ = 1 of 2 equal parts; $\frac{3}{4}$ = 3 of 4 equal parts.)

decimal— Any base-ten number that names a whole quantity and a fractional part. The numeral(s) to the right of the decimal point indicate the fractional part and the numeral(s) to the left of the decimal point indicate the whole numbers.

percent—One part of a whole that has been divided into 100 equal parts.

Go Figure

Name_____ Period_____ Date_____

Read and analyze.

Complete the following sentences.

1. To _____ means to make an educated guess based on certain information.

2. The sum of the values of a set of items divided by the number of items is the _____, or the _____.

3. A _____ is one part of a whole that has been divided into 100 equal parts.

4. A closed curved shape that has all points an equal distance from the center is called a _____.

5. _____ is the likelihood that a specific event or set of outcomes will occur.

6. The _____ is the amount of money subtracted from a selling price.

7. A _____ is straight, has no thickness, and continues in both directions without end.

8. A pair of numbers (x, y) that describes the location of a point on a coordinate plane is called an _____.

9. An _____ is one of the set of whole numbers, their opposites, and zero.

10. _____ is the science of thinking and proof by reasoning.

11. The ratio of the circumference of a circle to its diameter is called _____.

12. A _____ is a positive whole number greater than 1 that has only two factors, itself and 1.

13. _____ refers to terms or expressions that have equal value.

Communicate **Explain the strategies and thinking processes used to solve the problem(s).**

_____

_____

_____

_____

_____

_____

_____

Go Figure

Name_____ Period_____ Date_____

Think   Read and analyze.

Compute the area of the triangles and circles.

Formulas: Area of a triangle: $A = \frac{1}{2}bh$

Area of a circle: $A = \pi r^2$. Use 3.14 for π.

1.
5 cm
6.3 cm

_____

2.
8.7 cm

_____

3.
$13\frac{1}{4}$ in.
$11\frac{1}{2}$ in.

_____

4.
4 cm

_____

5.
8 in.

_____

6.
12.5 cm
13.2 cm

_____

7.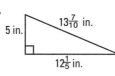
5 in. $13\frac{7}{10}$ in.
$12\frac{1}{5}$ in.

_____

8.
13 cm

_____

Solve   Show and label your work here.

_____
_____
_____
_____
_____
_____
_____
_____

Problem-solving plan...

Read			
Key words			
Analyze			
Add			
Subtract			
Multiply			
Divide			
Compare/ check			

Communicate   Explain the strategies and thinking processes used to solve the problem(s).

_____
_____
_____
_____
_____
_____

Vocabulary

area—The surface inside a closed two-dimensional figure or region.

circle—A closed curved shape that has all points an equal distance from the center.

triangle—A two-dimensional closed figure that has three sides and three angles.

formula—A recipe or equation used to solve a mathematical problem.

pi (π)—The ratio of the circumference of a circle to its diameter ($\pi \approx 3.14$ or $\frac{22}{7}$).

Go Figure

Name_____ Period_____ Date_____

Think   Read and analyze.

When Norah turned 16, she wanted to buy a car and a few extras, such as seat covers and a better radio. The price of the car was $5,500. She needed a loan to buy the car. She talked to two banks and found that the first bank would give her a loan for $6,300 and the second bank would give her a loan for $6,750.

A. How much more will Norah have to pay back if she takes the second loan?
_____

B. What is the difference between the price of the car and the first loan?
_____

C. What is the sum of the prices if she bought seat covers at $79, a radio at $495, and other odds and ends at $484? _____

Problem-solving plan...

Read			
Key words			
Analyze			
Add			
Subtract			
Multiply			
Divide			
Compare/ check			

Solve   Show and label your work here.

Communicate   Explain the strategies and thinking processes used to solve the problem(s).

Vocabulary

loan—An amount of money (usually lent at interest) that must be paid back.

Try This!

Go Figure

Name_____ Period_____ Date_____

Think Read and analyze.

Amanda's Electronics Shop is selling television sets for $399. With a 10% discount and a sales tax of 7.5%, what is the cost of a television set? _____

Problem-solving plan...

Read			
Key words			
Analyze			
Add			
Subtract			
Multiply			
Divide			
Compare/ check			

Solve Show and label your work here.

Communicate Explain the strategies and thinking processes used to solve the problem(s).

Vocabulary

This section may be used to introduce or reinforce any mathematical words or phrases.

_____

_____

_____

_____

_____

_____

Go Figure

Name_____ Period_____ Date_____

Think **Read and analyze.**

Devona had test scores of 86, 93, 79, 85, and 80. What score does she need on the next test to have an overall average of 85?_____

Problem-solving plan...

Read			
Key words			
Analyze			
Add			
Subtract			
Multiply			
Divide			
Compare/ check			

Solve **Show and label your work here.**

Communicate **Explain the strategies and thinking processes used to solve the problem(s).**

Vocabulary

average—The sum of the values of a set of items divided by the number of items.

Go Figure

Name_____ Period_____ Date_____

Think Read and analyze.

Latoya was in charge of buying monogrammed blouses for the cheerleaders. She bought 15 blouses for $14.95 apiece. She was charged an additional $12.75 in sales tax. She left the store with $13.00. How much money did she start with? _____

Problem-solving plan...

Read			
Key words			
Analyze			
Add			
Subtract			
Multiply			
Divide			
Compare/ check			

Solve Show and label your work here.

Communicate Explain the strategies and thinking processes used to solve the problem(s).

Vocabulary

sales tax—An amount of money for government use added to the cost of merchandise and collected at the place of sale.

Go Figure

Name_____ Period_____ Date_____

Think   Read and analyze.

Compute the volume of these rectangular prisms. $V = lwh$

1.

9 cm
9 cm
2.9 cm
_____

2.

9 cm
5.2 cm
2.1 cm
_____

3.
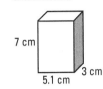
7 cm
3 cm
5.1 cm
_____

4.

9 cm
7.1 cm
5.4 cm
_____

5.
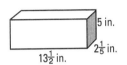
5 in.
$2\frac{1}{5}$ in.
$13\frac{1}{2}$ in.
_____

6.
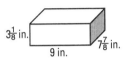
$3\frac{1}{8}$ in.
$7\frac{7}{8}$ in.
9 in.
_____

7.
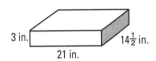
3 in.
$14\frac{1}{2}$ in.
21 in.
_____

8.

$3\frac{1}{5}$ in.
2 in.
$2\frac{1}{4}$ in.
_____

Solve   Show and label your work here.

Problem-solving plan...

Read			
Key words			
Analyze			
Add			
Subtract			
Multiply			
Divide			
Compare/ check			

Communicate   Explain the strategies and thinking processes used to solve the problem(s).

Vocabulary

volume—The measure of space inside a three-dimensional object. It is always labeled in cubic units.

rectangular prism—A solid figure whose sides are parallelograms and whose ends are parallel and alike in shape and size.

Go Figure

Name_____ Period_____ Date_____

Think — Read and analyze.

Maria bought a new monitor for her computer. The regular price of the monitor was $340, but $\frac{1}{4}$ of the price was discounted. Maria had three $100 bills to pay for her purchase. With the discount, how much money did Maria have left after buying the monitor?

_____

Problem-solving plan...

Read			
Key words			
Analyze			
Add			
Subtract			
Multiply			
Divide			
Compare/ check			

Solve — Show and label your work here.

Communicate — Explain the strategies and thinking processes used to solve the problem(s).

Vocabulary

discount—An amount of money subtracted from a selling price.

Go Figure

Name_____ Period_____ Date_____

Think   Read and analyze.

Jerome earned $7.25 per hour working at the Friendly Burger Hut. He wanted to earn enough money to buy a baseball jacket that cost $73.00 and a pennant that cost $12.50. In two days, he worked 14 hours. Taxes on his gross pay amounted to $8.75. Was Jerome's net pay enough for both purchases? If not, how much more did he need? If so, how much did he have left over?

_____

_____

Problem-solving plan...

Read			
Key words			
Analyze			
Add			
Subtract			
Multiply			
Divide			
Compare/ check			

Solve   Show and label your work here.

_____

_____

_____

_____

_____

_____

_____

_____

Communicate   Explain the strategies and thinking processes used to solve the problem(s).

_____

_____

_____

_____

_____

_____

_____

Vocabulary

gross pay—Total pay before deductions.

net pay—Amount of pay received after deductions (taxes, social security, etc.).

Try This!

Go Figure

Name_____ Period_____ Date_____

Think   Read and analyze.

A. Moi and her friend decided to drive across the United States on their vacation. They planned to drive an average of 300 miles a day and visit the sights as they went. The first day, they drove 222 miles. On the following days, they drove 312 miles, 410 miles, 150 miles, 275 miles, and 300 miles. How many miles do they need to drive the next day to meet their overall goal of an average of 300 miles a day? _____

_____

B. Prove your answer.

Problem-solving plan...

Read			
Key words			
Analyze			
Add			
Subtract			
Multiply			
Divide			
Compare/ check			

Solve   Show and label your work here.

Communicate   Explain the strategies and thinking processes used to solve the problem(s).

Vocabulary

This section may be used to introduce or reinforce any mathematical words or phrases.

_____

_____

_____

_____

_____

Go Figure

Name_____ Period_____ Date_____

Think   Read and analyze.

A. Jonsie was desperate for money. She borrowed $8 from her brother and $9 from her friend. She quickly paid back $5 to her brother and $7 to her friend. How much does she still owe? _____

B. No sooner had Jonsie repaid her brother and her friend some of what she owed than she borrowed another $5 from each of them. How much money does she owe now? _____

Problem-solving plan...

Read			
Key words			
Analyze			
Add			
Subtract			
Multiply			
Divide			
Compare/check			

Solve   Show and label your work here.

Communicate   Explain the strategies and thinking processes used to solve the problem(s).

Vocabulary

This section may be used to introduce or reinforce any mathematical words or phrases.

_____
_____
_____
_____
_____

Go Figure

Name_____ Period_____ Date_____

Think · Read and analyze.

Compute the perimeter of the polygons and the circumference of the circles.

Formulas: Perimeter of a triangle: P = s + s + s
Perimeter of a rectangle: P = 2l + 2w
Circumference of a circle: C = 2πr or πd. Use 3.14 for π.

Problem-solving plan...

Read			
Key words			
Analyze			
Add			
Subtract			
Multiply			
Divide			
Compare/check			

1. 5.2 cm, 2.5 cm

2. 9 in.

3. 5.22 in. 4.2 in. 3.1 in.

4. 3.7 in. 3.1 in. 4.2 in.

5. 22 cm

6. 5 in. $4\frac{1}{3}$ in. $3\frac{1}{3}$ in.

Solve · Show and label your work here.

Communicate · Explain the strategies and thinking processes used to solve the problem(s).

Vocabulary

perimeter—The distance around the outside of a two-dimensional shape.

polygon—A two-dimensional closed shape with three or more straight lines.

circumference—The distance around a circle.

circle—A closed curved shape that has all points an equal distance from the center.

triangle—A two-dimensional closed figure that has three sides and three angles.

rectangle—A parallelogram with four right angles.

pi (π)—The ratio of the circumference of a circle to its diameter (π ≈ 3.14 or $\frac{22}{7}$).

Go Figure

Name_____ Period_____ Date_____

Think — Read and analyze.

With great anticipation, the students in Mrs. Beakin's science class awaited the results of the state standards test. The students received the following scores:

92, 89, 45, 59, 52, 76, 46, 57, 75, 50, 72, 68, 63, 50, 48, 62

A. What is the median score for this science class? _____

B. Separate the data into quartiles and find the average for the first and fourth quartiles. _____

Problem-solving plan...

Read			
Key words			
Analyze			
Add			
Subtract			
Multiply			
Divide			
Compare/ check			

Solve — Show and label your work here.

Communicate — Explain the strategies and thinking processes used to solve the problem(s).

Vocabulary

median—The middle value in a distribution, above and below which lie an equal number of values.

data—Numerical information that can be represented in a graph, chart, or table.

quartile—One of the parts of a set of data that has been divided into four equal parts.

average—The sum of the values of a set of items divided by the number of items.

Go Figure

Name_____ Period_____ Date_____

Think   Read and analyze.

In an experiment, Abraham used a jar of buttons that contained well over 300 buttons that fell into the following color categories: white, red, blue, and green. There were the same number of buttons of each color. For the experiment, Abraham would close his eyes and randomly pick a button from the jar. He would make a note of the color of the button and put it back in the jar. On each of his first 3 picks, Abraham picked a red button. What is the probability that the next button he picks will be red? _____

Problem-solving plan...

Read			
Key words			
Analyze			
Add			
Subtract			
Multiply			
Divide			
Compare/ check			

Solve   Show and label your work here.

Communicate   Explain the strategies and thinking processes used to solve the problem(s).

Vocabulary

random—Having no predetermined pattern or plan; by chance.

probability—The likelihood that a specific event or set of outcomes will occur. It can be expressed as a ratio, fraction, decimal, or percent.

Go Figure

Name_____ Period_____ Date_____

Think   Read and analyze.

A. Latasha's literature class was told to read 150 pages for the test on Friday. On Monday she read 28 pages, on Tuesday 31, on Wednesday 38, and on Thursday 39. How many pages was she short of completing the assignment? _____

B. She read an average of _____ a day.

Problem-solving plan...

Read			
Key words			
Analyze			
Add			
Subtract			
Multiply			
Divide			
Compare/ check			

Solve   Show and label your work here.

Communicate   Explain the strategies and thinking processes used to solve the problem(s).

Vocabulary

average—The sum of the values of a set of items divided by the number of items.

Try This!

Go Figure

Name_____ Period_____ Date_____

Think   Read and analyze.

Sydney has 5 equal sets of small colored tiles. Each set is a different color: orange, purple, brown, yellow, and black. After placing the tiles in a large can and shaking them vigorously, she randomly picks a tile, notes its color, and puts it back in the can. She picks a yellow tile 4 times in a row. What are the chances that the next pick will be a yellow tile? _____

Problem-solving plan...

Read			
Key words			
Analyze			
Add			
Subtract			
Multiply			
Divide			
Compare/check			

Solve   Show and label your work here.

Communicate   Explain the strategies and thinking processes used to solve the problem(s).

Vocabulary

This section may be used to introduce or reinforce any mathematical words or phrases.

_____
_____
_____
_____
_____
_____

Go Figure

Name_____ Period_____ Date_____

Think   Read and analyze.

A. Using the table below, construct and label a circle graph showing the various pursuits of graduating seniors at Eagle High School.

**Pursuits of Graduating Seniors
Eagle High School**

Pursuit	%
Work	15
Four-year college	19
Two-year college	60
Other	6

Problem-solving plan...

Read			
Key words			
Analyze			
Add			
Subtract			
Multiply			
Divide			
Compare/ check			

B. In your circle graph, the number of seniors attending two-year colleges is _____ times greater than the number of seniors going to work.

Solve   Show and label your work here.

Communicate   Explain the strategies and thinking processes used to solve the problem(s).

Vocabulary

table—An arrangement of data for easy reference.

circle graph—A graph constructed in the shape of a circle showing the parts of a whole.

Go Figure

Name_____ Period_____ Date_____

Think   Read and analyze.

A plumber charges $35 for the first hour of work and $27 per hour for each additional hour. If Eduardo's plumbing bill is $170, how long did it take the plumber to complete the work? _____

Problem-solving plan...

Read			
Key words			
Analyze			
Add			
Subtract			
Multiply			
Divide			
Compare/ check			

Solve   Show and label your work here.

Communicate   Explain the strategies and thinking processes used to solve the problem(s).

Vocabulary

This section may be used to introduce or reinforce any mathematical words or phrases.

_____
_____
_____
_____
_____

80

Go Figure

Name_____ Period_____ Date_____

Think   Read and analyze.

Darwood's father gave Darwood a choice between two methods of payment for doing odd jobs around the house. The first choice was to get paid $4.75 every Saturday. The second choice was to get paid in increments for each day of the week. On Monday, he would get $0.04, on Tuesday $0.08, etc., the amount doubling each day through Sunday.

Problem-solving plan...

Read			
Key words			
Analyze			
Add			
Subtract			
Multiply			
Divide			
Compare/check			

1. Which is the better choice for Darwood? _____

2. What is the difference? _____

Solve   Show and label your work here.

Communicate   Explain the strategies and thinking processes used to solve the problem(s).

Vocabulary

increment—One of a series of regular, consecutive units.

difference—The answer to a subtraction problem.

double—To multiply by 2.

82

Name_____ Period_____ Date_____

Think — Read and analyze.

Compute the volume of these rectangular prisms. | V = lwh |

1. 9 in. 11¼ in. 7 in.

2. 11 cm 12 cm 9 cm

3. 4 in. 12½ in. 4 in.

4. 7.1 cm 7 cm 12 cm

_____ _____ _____ _____

5. 5′ 4′ 3′

6. 4 cm 2.1 cm 1.7 cm

7. 5 in. 12.5 in. 3 in.

8. 9 cm 3 cm 7.7 cm

_____ _____ _____ _____

Solve — Show and label your work here.

Problem-solving plan...

Read			
Key words			
Analyze			
Add			
Subtract			
Multiply			
Divide			
Compare/check			

Communicate — Explain the strategies and thinking processes used to solve the problem(s).

Vocabulary

volume—The measure of space inside a three-dimensional object. It is always labeled in cubic units.

rectangular prism—A solid figure whose sides are parallelograms and whose ends are parallel and alike in shape and size.

Go Figure

Name_____ Period_____ Date_____

Think   Read and analyze.

A. Ms. Gonzales finished grading the science exam. The class received 8 As,
14 Bs, 6 Cs, and 2 Ds. If a grade of A is equal to 4 points, a B grade is equal
to 3 points, a C to 2 points, and a D to 1 point, what is the average point
grade of the class? _____

B. Write the sentence that contains data that is irrelevant to the solution of
this problem. _____

_____

Problem-solving plan...

Read			
Key words			
Analyze			
Add			
Subtract			
Multiply			
Divide			
Compare/ check			

Solve   Show and label your work here.

Communicate   Explain the strategies and thinking processes used to solve
the problem(s).

Vocabulary

average—The sum of the
values of a set of items
divided by the number of
items.

Try This!

Name_____ Period_____ Date_____

Think   Read and analyze.

A. Would an employee at the Acme Book Company earn more if the pay was a flat $300 a week or if the pay started at $2.45 for all day Monday and tripled each day of the workweek through Friday? _____

_____

B. What does an employee earning $300 per week for a 5-day week earn per day? _____ Per month (4 weeks)? _____ Per year working 50 weeks? _____

Problem-solving plan...

Read			
Key words			
Analyze			
Add			
Subtract			
Multiply			
Divide			
Compare/ check			

Solve   Show and label your work here.

Communicate   Explain the strategies and thinking processes used to solve the problem(s).

Vocabulary

This section may be used to introduce or reinforce any mathematical words or phrases.

_____

_____

_____

_____

_____

_____

Go Figure

Name_____ Period_____ Date_____

Think and Solve Read and analyze.

Hank's Car Wash wants to know how to schedule its personnel. Hank collected the following information about how many cars were washed during a one-week period: Monday 162, Tuesday 204, Wednesday 173, Thursday 212, Friday 275, Saturday 295, and Sunday 150.

A. On the grid below, construct a graph showing the number of cars washed each day of the week. Give your graph a title and label the axes.

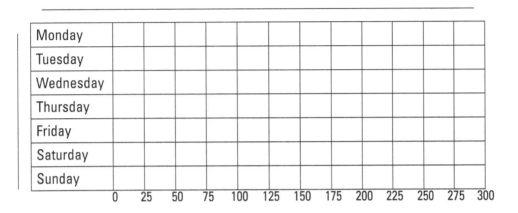

B. Tell what the horizontal axis measures. _____
   Tell what the vertical axis represents. _____

C. On what two days does Hank need the most employees? _____

D. If Hank goes to a 5-day workweek, which days should he close? Explain._____

_____

_____

Communicate Explain the strategies and thinking processes used to solve the problem(s).

_____

_____

_____

_____

_____

_____

Vocabulary

grid—A framework of horizontal and vertical lines that form squares for graphing information.

horizontal axis—The scale on the bottom of a graph.

vertical axis—The scale on the left side of a graph.

Go Figure

Name_____ Period_____ Date_____

Write definitions for the following words.

1. average _____
   _____

2. mode _____
   _____

3. thousands place _____
   _____
   _____

4. numerator _____
   _____

5. sequence _____
   _____

6. tens place _____
   _____
   _____

7. simplest form _____
   _____

8. factor _____
   _____

9. quartile _____
   _____

10. net pay _____
    _____

Go Figure

Name_____ Period_____ Date_____

Think and Solve Read and analyze.

A. Use the $\frac{1}{4}$-inch grid below to draw a right triangle (△ABC) with legs that are $1\frac{3}{4}$ inches and $1\frac{1}{2}$ inches.

B. Label the legs and the hypotenuse.

Problem-solving plan...

Read			
Key words			
Analyze			
Add			
Subtract			
Multiply			
Divide			
Compare/ check			

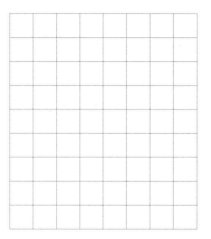

Communicate Explain the strategies and thinking processes used to solve the problem(s).

_____

_____

_____

_____

_____

_____

Vocabulary

right triangle—A triangle that has a right angle (90°).

leg—One of the two sides of a right triangle that form the right angle.

hypotenuse—The longest side of a right triangle. It is opposite the right angle.

Go Figure

Name _____ Period _____ Date _____

Think   Read and analyze.

This is a permutation problem.

Cecile is a camp counselor, and she is planning the camp schedule. The activities are tennis, horseback riding, archery, hiking, and nature study. She can arrange the activities in any order. How many ways can she put the five activities in order? _____

Problem-solving plan...

Read			
Key words			
Analyze			
Add			
Subtract			
Multiply			
Divide			
Compare/check			

Solve   Show and label your work here.

Communicate   Explain the strategies and thinking processes used to solve the problem(s).

Vocabulary

permutation—An ordered arrangement of all or some of the items of a set.

Go Figure

Name_____ Period_____ Date_____

Read and analyze.

When the History Museum opened, the city kept careful records of attendance. In the first month, 2,500 people visited the museum. In the second month, attendance went up to 2,840 visitors. During the third month, 250 fewer people visited than in the second month. How many people altogether visited the museum during the three-month period? _____

Problem-solving plan...

Read			
Key words			
Analyze			
Add			
Subtract			
Multiply			
Divide			
Compare/ check			

Solve **Show and label your work here.**

Communicate **Explain the strategies and thinking processes used to solve the problem(s).**

Vocabulary

This section may be used to introduce or reinforce any mathematical words or phrases.

_____
_____
_____
_____
_____
_____

Try This!   # Go Figure

Name_____ Period_____ Date_____

Think   Read and analyze.

1. Use the $\frac{1}{4}$-inch grid below to show how two right triangles of the same size can occupy the total space provided.

Problem-solving plan...

Read			
Key words			
Analyze			
Add			
Subtract			
Multiply			
Divide			
Compare/ check			

2. What is the length in inches of the longer leg of each triangle?
_____

3. What is the length in inches of the shorter leg? _____

4. What is the perimeter of this parallelogram? _____

5. What is the area of each right triangle (A = $\frac{1}{2}$bh)? _____

Solve   Show and label your work here.

Communicate   Explain the strategies and thinking processes used to solve the problem(s).

Vocabulary

This section may be used to introduce or reinforce any mathematical words or phrases.

_____

_____

_____

_____

_____

_____

Go Figure

Name_____ Period_____ Date_____

Think Read and analyze.

Eduardo, Ron, and Myra all cashed checks for the same amount of money at the beginning of the week. At the end of the week, Eduardo had spent $\frac{3}{4}$ of his money, Ron had spent $\frac{7}{8}$, and Myra $\frac{4}{5}$.

A. Express the amounts each person spent in fractions with the lowest common denominator. _____

_____

B. Use the < or > symbol to show who spent the greater amount of money and who spent less.

Ron _____ Myra   Eduardo _____ Ron   Myra _____ Eduardo

C. Draw a representation to show what part of the money each person spent.

Problem-solving plan...

Read			
Key words			
Analyze			
Add			
Subtract			
Multiply			
Divide			
Compare/ check			

Solve Show and label your work here.

Communicate Explain the strategies and thinking processes used to solve the problem(s).

Vocabulary

symbol—A picture or shape that stands for an idea or word(s): < = less than (6 < 9); > = greater than (5 > 3).

representation—A picture that shows a mathematical idea or relationship.

Go Figure

Name_____ Period_____ Date_____

Think   Read and analyze.

Paulette had the responsibility of baking cookies for the debate team picnic. After giving each member of the team 9 cookies, she had 6 cookies left. She wanted to give 1 more cookie to each member, but she realized that she was 1 cookie short. How many cookies did she bake? _____

Problem-solving plan...

Read			
Key words			
Analyze			
Add			
Subtract			
Multiply			
Divide			
Compare/ check			

Solve   Show and label your work here.

Communicate   Explain the strategies and thinking processes used to solve the problem(s).

Vocabulary

This section may be used to introduce or reinforce any mathematical words or phrases.

_____

_____

_____

_____

_____

Go Figure

Name_____ Period_____ Date_____

Think and Solve Read and analyze.

A. Define and draw the following geometric figures.

1. equilateral triangle _____
_____
_____

2. rectangle _____
_____
_____

3. obtuse angle _____
_____
_____

4. acute angle _____
_____
_____

5. rhombus _____
_____
_____

6. bisected acute angle_____
_____
_____

B. In which of the above figures do the angles equal 360°?

_____

Problem-solving plan...

Read			
Key words			
Analyze			
Add			
Subtract			
Multiply			
Divide			
Compare/ check			

Communicate Explain the strategies and thinking processes used to solve the problem(s).

_____
_____
_____
_____
_____
_____
_____
_____

Vocabulary

This section may be used to introduce or reinforce any mathematical words or phrases.

_____
_____
_____
_____
_____
_____

Go Figure

Name_____ Period_____ Date_____

Think   Read and analyze.

Marla decided to start a summer housecleaning business. The first summer she had 3 summer-long customers. Because she was very good and very dependable, word soon got around. The next summer she had twice as many customers. By the third summer, she had 5 times as many customers as the first summer.

A. What was the total number of customers Marla had during the first three summers of her business? _____

B. If she earned a profit of $210 from each customer over a summer, how much profit did she earn over all three summers? _____

Problem-solving plan...

Read			
Key words			
Analyze			
Add			
Subtract			
Multiply			
Divide			
Compare/ check			

Solve   Show and label your work here.

Communicate   Explain the strategies and thinking processes used to solve the problem(s).

Vocabulary

profit—The amount of money gained in excess of the original cost.

Go Figure

Name_____ Period_____ Date_____

Think   Read and analyze.

On the planet of Berneria, the area of the Morgue Sea is 15,800 square miles, which is 1,800 square miles more than 4 times the area of Lake Oboe. What is the area of Lake Oboe? _____

Problem-solving plan...

Read			
Key words			
Analyze			
Add			
Subtract			
Multiply			
Divide			
Compare/check			

Solve   Show and label your work here.

Communicate   Explain the strategies and thinking processes used to solve the problem(s).

Vocabulary

area—The surface inside a closed two-dimensional figure or region.

Try This!

Go Figure

Name_____ Period_____ Date_____

Think   Read and analyze.

The Big Track Tire Factory supplied tires for drivers at the Cyclone Raceway. The factory's deliveryman delivered 7 tires for each driver and had 21 tires left on the truck. He went back to the factory to pick up 14 more tires so that each driver would have 2 full sets of 4 tires.

A. How many tires were on the truck for the first delivery?

_____

B. What was the total number of tires delivered? _____

Problem-solving plan...

Read			
Key words			
Analyze			
Add			
Subtract			
Multiply			
Divide			
Compare/ check			

Solve   Show and label your work here.

_____
_____
_____
_____
_____
_____
_____
_____
_____

Communicate   Explain the strategies and thinking processes used to solve the problem(s).

_____
_____
_____
_____
_____
_____
_____

Vocabulary

This section may be used to introduce or reinforce any mathematical words or phrases.

_____

_____

_____

_____

_____

_____

Go Figure

Name_____ Period_____ Date_____

Think   Read and analyze.

Elanora the unlucky chipmunk fell into a muddy ditch 2 meters deep. She climbed $\frac{1}{2}$ of a meter each hour and then stopped to rest for a moment. Unfortunately, when she was resting after each hour of climbing, she slid back $\frac{1}{4}$ of a meter.

A. Not counting the time she rested, how long did it take Elanora to get out of the ditch? _____

B. Draw a representation to solve this problem.

Problem-solving plan...

Read			
Key words			
Analyze			
Add			
Subtract			
Multiply			
Divide			
Compare/ check			

Solve   Show and label your work here.

Communicate   Explain the strategies and thinking processes used to solve the problem(s).

Vocabulary

meter—The basic unit of length in the metric system. It is equivalent to 39.37 inches, or a little more than 3 feet.

representation—A picture that shows a mathematical idea or relationship.

Go Figure

Name_____ Period_____ Date_____

Think Read and analyze.

A. Ronald's job as a managing editor is to assign his team to various tasks. A project they are working on requires 4 editors, 5 computer operators, 2 proofreaders, 3 artists, and 1 layout person. He will assign each of the employees to the project for 20 hours a week for 3 weeks. Editors make $18 an hour, computer operators make $15, proofreaders make $16, artists make $14, and the layout person makes $21. Complete the table below to show how Ronald organized the project.

B. What is the total cost of labor for the project? _____

C. How many total labor hours were required to complete the project? _____

Problem-solving plan...

Read			
Key words			
Analyze			
Add			
Subtract			
Multiply			
Divide			
Compare/check			

Solve Show and label your work here.

A.

Employees	Salary per Hour	Number of Employees per Task	Total Project Hours per Employee	Total Project Hours Worked per Task	Total Project Cost per Task
Totals					

Communicate Explain the strategies and thinking processes used to solve the problem(s).

Vocabulary

table—An arrangement of data for easy reference.

98

Go Figure

Name_____ Period_____ Date_____

Think Read and analyze.

Find the missing angle measurement for each triangle. (The sum of the measurements of the angles of a triangle equals 180°.)

1.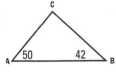

_____

2.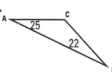

_____

3.

_____

4.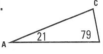

_____

5.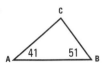

_____

6.

_____

7.

_____

8.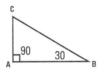

_____

Solve Show and label your work here.

Problem-solving plan...

Read			
Key words			
Analyze			
Add			
Subtract			
Multiply			
Divide			
Compare/ check			

Communicate Explain the strategies and thinking processes used to solve the problem(s).

Vocabulary

angle—A shape formed by two rays with a common point of origin (vertex).

triangle—A two-dimensional closed figure that has three sides and three angles.

sum—The answer to an addition problem.

100

Name _____ Period _____ Date _____

Think — Read and analyze.

Martha found just the necklace she was looking for at Sally's Classic Jewelry Store. The sale price was discounted 20% off the original price of $49.95. The sales tax was 7.5%. What was the final cost of the necklace? _____

Problem-solving plan...

Read			
Key words			
Analyze			
Add			
Subtract			
Multiply			
Divide			
Compare/check			

Solve — Show and label your work here.

Communicate — Explain the strategies and thinking processes used to solve the problem(s).

Vocabulary

discount—An amount of money subtracted from a selling price.

sales tax—An amount of money for government use added to the cost of merchandise and collected at the place of sale.

Go Figure

Name_____ Period_____ Date_____

Read and analyze.

Fill in the blanks to make each sentence correct.

1. _____ is the distance around a circle.

2. The _____, in terms of geometry, generally refers to the side on which a figure rests.

3. _____, when added, equal 90 degrees.

4. _____ is another word (synonym) for average.

5. In a list of values arranged from lowest to highest or highest to lowest (ordered), the _____ is the middle number or the average of the two middle numbers.

6. _____ is the likelihood of something occurring.

7. _____ is a way to represent part of a whole that has been divided into 100 equal pieces.

8. _____ is the distance around the outside of a two-dimensional shape.

9. _____ is the ratio of the circumference of a circle to its diameter.

10. A _____ is a positive whole number greater than 1 that has only two factors, itself and 1.

11. An _____ is a pair of numbers (x, y) that describes the location of a point on a grid.

12. A _____ is a set of perpendicular number lines that intersect at their zero points (the point of origin). The horizontal line is called the _____ -axis and the vertical line is called the _____ -axis.

Name_____ Period_____ Date_____

Think — Read and analyze.

The Creative Garden Center has contracted with the city to design and build a small lighted park and recreation area. The job is estimated to cost $38,500 and must be completed in 15 days. The project will employ 2 landscape designers at $35 per hour, each working 8 hours; 4 gardeners at $10 per hour, each working 42 hours; 2 carpenters at $23 per hour, each working 55 hours; 1 electrician at $30 per hour, working 50 hours; and 2 sprinkler system installers at $20 per hour, each working 32 hours.

Problem-solving plan...

Read			
Key words			
Analyze			
Add			
Subtract			
Multiply			
Divide			
Compare/ check			

A. Complete the table using the above information, making columns for job categories, number of workers per job category, hours per worker, total hours worked per job category, hourly pay, and total labor cost per job category. Also have totals for the appropriate columns.

B. How many people in all worked on the project? _____

C. What was the average hourly cost for labor for this project? _____

D. If the materials for the park cost $17,200, what was the profit for the project? _____

E. What percentage of the total contract price went to labor? _____

Solve — Show and label your work here.

Job Category					
Totals					

Communicate — Explain the strategies and thinking processes used to solve the problem(s).

_____

_____

_____

Vocabulary

This section may be used to introduce or reinforce any mathematical words or phrases.

_____

_____

_____

_____

Go Figure

Name_____ Period_____ Date_____

Think and Solve   Read and analyze.

Refer to the graphs below and then answer the questions.

**Graph A
Changes in Interest Rates
1999–2003**

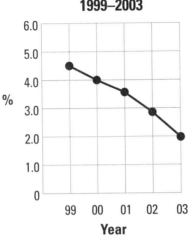

**Graph B
Changes in Interest Rates
1999–2003**

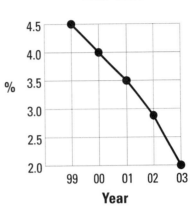

A. Explain why the representation of these data in one of the graphs gives a more dramatic picture of the interest rates from 1999 to 2003._____

_____

_____

B. Tell why the press might be more likely to print Graph B in a newspaper article. _____

_____

_____

C. In comparing these graphs, what lesson can be learned about graphic representation?

_____

_____

Communicate   Explain the strategies and thinking processes used to solve the problem(s).

Vocabulary

graph (*n*)—A visual representation of information or data.

data—Numerical information that can be used in making a graph, chart, or table.

interest rate—A charge for a loan, usually a percentage of the amount of the loan.

Go Figure

Name_____ Period_____ Date_____

Read and analyze.

A. If Sylvia had a score of $\frac{7}{10}$ on the science quiz, what was her score as a percent? _____

B. On the science midterm, Willard's score was 85%. Show his score as a fraction in its simplest form. _____

Problem-solving plan...

Read			
Key words			
Analyze			
Add			
Subtract			
Multiply			
Divide			
Compare/ check			

Solve **Show and label your work here.**

Communicate **Explain the strategies and thinking processes used to solve the problem(s).**

Vocabulary

percent—One part of a whole that has been divided into 100 equal parts.

fraction—A part of one whole unit. ($\frac{1}{2}$ = 1 of 2 equal parts; $\frac{3}{4}$ = 3 of 4 equal parts.)

simplest form— A fraction reduced to its lowest terms. ($\frac{3}{6} = \frac{1}{2}$; $\frac{5}{25} = \frac{1}{5}$)

Go Figure

Name_____ Period_____ Date_____

Think   Read and analyze.

A. Geoffrey's father is buying a new car. He likes a model called the Beagle. For the paint color, Geoffrey's father can choose from among 10 colors. For the racing stripe, he has a choice of 6 colors. For the upholstery, he can choose from among 5 colors. From among these choices, he can choose whatever colors he likes for the paint, stripe, and upholstery. How many different color combinations are there? _____

B. This problem is called a _____ problem.

Problem-solving plan...

Read			
Key words			
Analyze			
Add			
Subtract			
Multiply			
Divide			
Compare/check			

Solve   Show and label your work here.

Communicate   Explain the strategies and thinking processes used to solve the problem(s).

Vocabulary

permutation—An ordered arrangement of all or some of the items of a set.

combination—The result of putting two or more things together.

Name_____ Period_____ Date_____

Think Read and analyze.

$$V = lwh$$

What is the volume of a rectangular solid whose length (l) = 3 feet, width (w) = 1.5 feet, and height (h) = 2 feet?

_____

2 ft

1.5 ft

3 ft

Problem-solving plan...

Read			
Key words			
Analyze			
Add			
Subtract			
Multiply			
Divide			
Compare/ check			

Solve Show and label your work here.

Communicate Explain the strategies and thinking processes used to solve the problem(s).

Vocabulary

volume—The measure of the space inside a three-dimensional object. It is always labeled in cubic units.

rectangular solid—A solid figure whose sides are a parallelogram and whose ends are parallel and alike in shape and size.

Go Figure

Name_____ Period_____ Date_____

Think — Read and analyze.

Kameron bought 9 more books for his college courses than Rudy did. Together they bought 17 books. How many did each buy?

_____

Problem-solving plan...

Read			
Key words			
Analyze			
Add			
Subtract			
Multiply			
Divide			
Compare/ check			

Solve — Show and label your work here.

Communicate — Explain the strategies and thinking processes used to solve the problem(s).

Vocabulary

This section may be used to introduce or reinforce any mathematical words or phrases.

_____

_____

_____

_____

_____

_____

Go Figure

Name _____ Period _____ Date _____

Think   Read and analyze.

The formula for finding the volume of a rectangular solid is V = lwh.

A. Modify this formula to find the formula of a triangular prism. What is the formula?

_____

B. Find the volume of a triangular prism whose length (l) is 4 feet, width (w) is 2.5 feet, and height (h) is 1.5 feet. _____

Problem-solving plan...			
Read			
Key words			
Analyze			
Add			
Subtract			
Multiply			
Divide			
Compare/ check			

Solve   Show and label your work here.

_____

_____

_____

_____

_____

_____

Communicate   Explain the strategies and thinking processes used to solve the problem(s).

_____

_____

_____

_____

_____

_____

Vocabulary

This section may be used to introduce or reinforce any mathematical words or phrases.

_____

_____

_____

_____

_____

_____

Go Figure

Name_____ Period_____ Date_____

Think   Read and analyze.

A. When Chad went to the campus bookstore, he found a secondhand chemistry book for $10.50, a used algebra book for $15.50, and a very old sociology book with notes written in it for $12.00. All he could find for his English class was a new book that cost $42.75. The sales tax is 7.0%. How much did Chad pay in total for his books? _____

B. Chad had budgeted $75.00 for books. Did he have enough? How much did he have left over or how much more did he need? _____

_____

Problem-solving plan...

Read			
Key words			
Analyze			
Add			
Subtract			
Multiply			
Divide			
Compare/ check			

Solve   Show and label your work here.

Communicate   Explain the strategies and thinking processes used to solve the problem(s).

Vocabulary

sales tax—An amount of money for government use added to the cost of an item and collected at the place of sale.

budget—A plan for meeting expenses.

Go Figure

Name_____ Period_____ Date_____

Think Read and analyze.

Walt took care of his sister's dog when she moved to a new city that was 440 miles from his house. When she wanted her dog back, he offered to meet her halfway. They leave their houses at the same time and drive straight through. If Walt drives 60 miles per hour (mph) and his sister drives 50 mph, how long will it be before they meet? _____

$$time = \frac{distance}{rate}$$

Problem-solving plan...

Read			
Key words			
Analyze			
Add			
Subtract			
Multiply			
Divide			
Compare/ check			

Solve Show and label your work here.

Communicate Explain the strategies and thinking processes used to solve the problem(s).

Vocabulary

distance—The measurement between two points.

rate—A quantity, amount, or degree measured by some standard (in this case, speed).

Go Figure

Name_____ Period_____ Date_____

Think and Solve Read and analyze.

Scatter plots are used to show the relationship between two sets of related data. Pairs of data from the sets are graphed as points. The points are not connected.

The correlation key indicates whether the relationship between the two sets of data is positive, negative, or zero.

Problem-solving plan...

Read			
Key words			
Analyze			
Add			
Subtract			
Multiply			
Divide			
Compare/ check			

A. Using the data provided for one week, construct a scatter plot comparing individual customers' incomes and the prices of the cars they purchased.

	Income ($)	Price of Car Purchased ($)
1.	5,000	1,500
2.	53,000	28,000
3.	30,000	25,000
4.	10,000	8,000
5.	19,000	9,500
6.	85,000	55,000
7.	72,000	38,000
8.	45,000	35,000
9.	68,000	41,000
10.	46,000	23,000

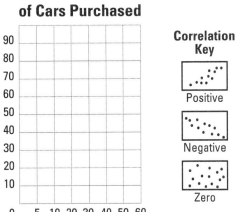

Income and Price of Cars Purchased

Correlation Key

Positive

Negative

Zero

B. Look at the scatter plot and the correlation key above. Write two observations.

_____

_____

_____

_____

_____

Vocabulary

scatter plot—A method of graphing sets of related data by placing points (dots) on a graph to compare the sets.

set—A collection of objects or numbers.

relationship—The connection between identified variables.

data—Numerical information that can be used in making a graph.

graph (*v*)— To make a visual representation of information or data.

correlation—The relationship between two sets of numerical values.

Communicate Explain the strategies and thinking processes used to solve the problem(s).

....

....

....

....

....

Go Figure

Name_____ Period_____ Date_____

Think — Read and analyze.

What is the probability of tossing a penny 4 times and getting 4 tails in a row? _____

Problem-solving plan...

Read			
Key words			
Analyze			
Add			
Subtract			
Multiply			
Divide			
Compare/check			

Solve — Show and label your work here.

Communicate — Explain the strategies and thinking processes used to solve the problem(s).

Vocabulary

probability—The likelihood that a specific event or set of outcomes will occur. It can be expressed as a ratio, fraction, decimal, or percent.

Go Figure

Name_____ Period_____ Date_____

Think — Read and analyze.

Pythagorean theorem: In a right triangle, the sum of the squares of the legs (a and b) equals the square of the hypotenuse (c): $a^2 + b^2 = c^2$.

Therefore, $c^2 - a^2 = b^2$ and $c^2 - b^2 = a^2$.

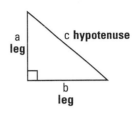

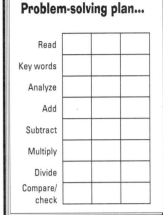

Problem-solving plan...

Read			
Key words			
Analyze			
Add			
Subtract			
Multiply			
Divide			
Compare/ check			

A. In a right triangle, if a = 4 and b = 3, what does c equal? _____

B. The longest side of a right triangle is called the _____.

C. In a right triangle, what is the length of b when c = 12 feet and a = 9 feet? _____
Give the formula and draw a representation for this question.

Solve — Show and label your work here.

_____
_____
_____
_____
_____
_____
_____
_____

Communicate — Explain the strategies and thinking processes used to solve the problem(s).

_____
_____
_____
_____
_____
_____

Vocabulary

theorem—A statement of truth or an idea that can be proved.

Pythagorean theorem—A statement of truth discovered by Pythagoras, a Greek mathematician born about 500 B.C.

right triangle—A triangle that has one right angle (90°).

leg—One of the two sides of a right triangle that form the right angle.

hypotenuse—The longest side of a right triangle. It is opposite the right angle.

square (*v*)—To multiply a number by itself (3^2 means $3 \times 3 = 9$; 5^2 means $5 \times 5 = 25$).

representation—A picture that shows a mathematical idea or relationship.

formula—A recipe or equation used to solve a mathematical problem.

Go Figure

Name_____ Period_____ Date_____

Think   Read and analyze.

An airplane flying at 260 miles an hour leaves California for New York. At the same time, a plane departs from New York for California flying at 340 miles an hour.

A. If the flying distance between New York and California is approximately 2,400 miles, how long will it take for the planes to pass each other? _____

B. How long will it take each plane to reach its destination?

New York–bound plane: _____

California-bound plane: _____

Problem-solving plan...

Read			
Key words			
Analyze			
Add			
Subtract			
Multiply			
Divide			
Compare/ check			

Solve   Show and label your work here.

Communicate   Explain the strategies and thinking processes used to solve the problem(s).

Vocabulary

This section may be used to introduce or reinforce any mathematical words or phrases.

_____

_____

_____

_____

_____

Go Figure

Name_____ Period_____ Date_____

Think   Read and analyze.

The formula for the volume of a cone is $V = \frac{1}{3}\pi r^2 h$. Use 3.14 for π.

A. Compute the volume of cones with the following measurements.

1. r = 3 in., h = 10 in. _____

2. r = 2 ft, h = 14 ft _____

3. r = 5 in., h = 18 in. _____

4. r = 6 ft, h = 21 ft _____

B. If the volume of a cone is $\frac{1}{3}$ the volume of a cylinder with the same dimensions, what is the volume of a cylinder when the volume of the cone is 92.11 in.^{3}? _____

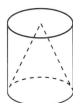

Problem-solving plan...

Read			
Key words			
Analyze			
Add			
Subtract			
Multiply			
Divide			
Compare/ check			

Solve   Show and label your work here.

_____
_____
_____
_____
_____
_____
_____
_____
_____

Communicate   Explain the strategies and thinking processes used to solve the problem(s).

_____
_____
_____
_____
_____
_____

Vocabulary

formula—A recipe or equation used to solve a mathematical problem.

volume—The measure of space inside a three-dimensional object. It is always labeled in cubic units.

cone—A solid or hollow figure with a flat round base that tapers evenly to a point at the top.

cylinder—A round, long solid or hollow figure with flat circular ends.

dimension—A measurement, especially of height, width, or length.

Go Figure

Name_____ Period_____ Date_____

Think   Read and analyze.

Anthony took his St. Bernard to the pet store. He bought a 40-lb bag of Super Kibble for $36.98, a rubber bone for $7.59, and a huge collar for $18.75. If the sales tax was 7.5%, what was the total cost for the pet supplies? _____

Problem-solving plan...

Read			
Key words			
Analyze			
Add			
Subtract			
Multiply			
Divide			
Compare/ check			

Solve   Show and label your work here.

Communicate   Explain the strategies and thinking processes used to solve the problem(s).

Vocabulary

sales tax—An amount of money for government use added to the cost of merchandise and collected at the place of sale.

Go Figure

Name_____ Period_____ Date_____

Think   Read and analyze.

A. A new strain of flu virus was introduced into a small mountain community by a tourist. On the first day, 2 people were exposed to the virus. On each succeeding day, the number of people exposed tripled. The entire town had been exposed on the ninth day. How many people live in the town?

_____

B. If all the people in the community were exposed on the ninth day, on what day was $\frac{1}{3}$ of the community exposed? _____

Problem-solving plan...

Read			
Key words			
Analyze			
Add			
Subtract			
Multiply			
Divide			
Compare/ check			

Solve   Show and label your work here.

Communicate   Explain the strategies and thinking processes used to solve the problem(s).

Vocabulary

triple—To multiply by 3.

Go Figure

Name_____ Period_____ Date_____

Think — Read and analyze.

Ricardo's grandfather is 64 years old. He is 10 years older than 3 times Ricardo's age. How old is Ricardo? Write this problem in equation form and solve it. Check your answer.

_____

Problem-solving plan...

Read			
Key words			
Analyze			
Add			
Subtract			
Multiply			
Divide			
Compare/check			

Solve — Show and label your work here.

_____
_____
_____
_____
_____
_____
_____
_____
_____

Communicate — Explain the strategies and thinking processes used to solve the problem(s).

_____
_____
_____
_____
_____
_____
_____

Vocabulary

equation—A mathematical sentence that has two equivalent expressions separated by an equal sign.

Go Figure

Name_____ Period_____ Date_____

Think   Read and analyze.

Out of 50 students, 10 were to be selected to receive a free trip to Washington, D.C. Each of the 50 students randomly drew a ticket from a bowl of tickets numbered 1 through 50. The students who drew tickets 41 though 50 would win the trip.

A. What is the probability of a student winning? _____

B. If 15 students were being selected out of 120, what is the probability of a student winning? _____

Problem-solving plan...

Read			
Key words			
Analyze			
Add			
Subtract			
Multiply			
Divide			
Compare/check			

Solve   Show and label your work here.

Communicate   Explain the strategies and thinking processes used to solve the problem(s).

Vocabulary

random—Having no predetermined pattern or plan; by chance.

probability—The likelihood that a specific event or set of outcomes will occur. It can be expressed as a ratio, fraction, decimal, or percent.

Try This!

Go Figure

Name_____ Period_____ Date_____

Think Read and analyze.

Gary ate one-half of a quesadilla. His sister ate one-third of what was left.

A. How much of the quesadilla was eaten? _____

B. How much of the quesadilla was left over? _____

C. Make a representation to illustrate your solution.

Problem-solving plan...

Read			
Key words			
Analyze			
Add			
Subtract			
Multiply			
Divide			
Compare/ check			

Solve Show and label your work here.

Communicate Explain the strategies and thinking processes used to solve the problem(s).

Vocabulary

This section may be used to introduce or reinforce any mathematical words or phrases.

_____

_____

_____

_____

_____

_____

Go Figure

Name_____ Period_____ Date_____

Think — Read and analyze.

When Holly was 10 years old, her parents started putting $125 a month into a mutual fund for her. Her grandfather contributes $25 a month, and Holly adds $15 each month. How much money will have been put into the fund by Holly's 25th birthday? _____

Problem-solving plan...

Read			
Key words			
Analyze			
Add			
Subtract			
Multiply			
Divide			
Compare/ check			

Solve — Show and label your work here.

Communicate — Explain the strategies and thinking processes used to solve the problem(s).

Vocabulary

mutual fund—An investment company that invests the money of its shareholders in a variety of stocks and bonds.

Go Figure

Name_____ Period_____ Date_____

Think   Read and analyze.

Test your logic with this problem.

A. Carol from Rose Garden Florists delivered roses to three of her customers on Saturday. Compute the number of roses she delivered to each customer and construct a table using the following information.

3 dozen roses to the church
9 dozen roses altogether to the hospital and the nursing home
8 dozen roses altogether to the church and the hospital

B. Which customer received the most flowers? _____

C. Which customer received the fewest flowers? _____

D. How many individual flowers were delivered? _____

Problem-solving plan...

Read			
Key words			
Analyze			
Add			
Subtract			
Multiply			
Divide			
Compare/ check			

Solve   Show and label your work here.

Communicate   Explain the strategies and thinking processes used to solve the problem(s).

Vocabulary

logic—The science of sound thinking and proof by reasoning.

table—An arrangement of data for easy reference.

Go Figure

Name_____ Period_____ Date_____

Think   Read and analyze.

Jeronna had set aside $125 for school clothes. From this amount, she had already spent $35 for a jacket. She went to the One Price Dress Shop, where all items were $15. How many items could she buy? _____ Show two ways of solving this problem.

Problem-solving plan...

Read			
Key words			
Analyze			
Add			
Subtract			
Multiply			
Divide			
Compare/ check			

Solve   Show and label your work here.

Communicate   Explain the strategies and thinking processes used to solve the problem(s).

Vocabulary

This section may be used to introduce or reinforce any mathematical words or phrases.

_____

_____

_____

_____

_____

123

Go Figure

Name_____ Period_____ Date_____

Think   **Read and analyze.**

The formula for the volume of a cylinder is $V = \pi r^2 h$. Use 3.14 for π.

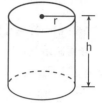

A. Compute the volume of cylinders with the following measurements.

1. r = 5 ft, h = 15 ft _____   2. r = 3 in., h = 5 in. _____
3. r = 7.5 in., h = 8 in. _____ 4. r = 4 cm, h = 6 cm _____

B. If the volume of a cone is $\frac{1}{3}$ the volume of a cylinder with the same dimensions, what is the volume of a cone when the volume of the cylinder is 791.28 in.^{3}? _____

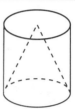

Solve   **Show and label your work here.**

_____

_____

_____

_____

_____

_____

_____

_____

_____

Problem-solving plan...			
Read			
Key words			
Analyze			
Add			
Subtract			
Multiply			
Divide			
Compare/ check			

Communicate   Explain the strategies and thinking processes used to solve the problem(s).

_____

_____

_____

_____

_____

_____

Vocabulary

formula—A recipe or equation used to solve a mathematical problem.

volume—The measure of space inside a three-dimensional object. It is always labeled in cubic units.

cylinder—A round, long solid or hollow figure with flat circular ends.

cone—A solid or hollow figure with a flat round base that tapers evenly to a point at the top.

dimension—A measurement, especially of height, width, or length.

Go Figure

Name_____ Period_____ Date_____

Think **Read and analyze.**

A. Ilsa is employed selling automobiles at a dealership. She receives a 4.3% commission on each automobile she sells. The rest of the selling price goes to the dealership. What is the selling price of a car if the dealer gets $28,000? Round off your answer to the nearest dollar. _____

B. What is the amount of Ilsa's commission to the nearest dollar? _____

Problem-solving plan...

Read			
Key words			
Analyze			
Add			
Subtract			
Multiply			
Divide			
Compare/ check			

Solve **Show and label your work here.**

Communicate **Explain the strategies and thinking processes used to solve the problem(s).**

Vocabulary

commission—A fee or percentage given to a salesperson for services.

Try This!

Name_____ Period_____ Date_____

Think **Read and analyze.**

Mario deposited the following amounts in his bank account: January $165.00, February $129.00, March $89.00, April $93.00, May $83.00, June $29.00, July $53.50, August $40.00, September $56.00, October $105.00, November $78.00, and December $133.00.

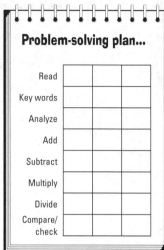

Problem-solving plan...

Read			
Key words			
Analyze			
Add			
Subtract			
Multiply			
Divide			
Compare/ check			

A. On the grid below, draw a line graph to show Mario's deposits.

B. What was Mario's total deposit for the year? _____

C. What was Mario's average monthly deposit for the year?

_____

Solve **Show and label your work here.**

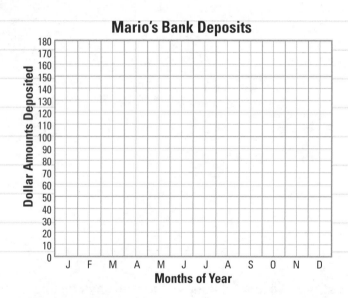

Mario's Bank Deposits

Communicate **Explain the strategies and thinking processes used to solve the problem(s).**

_____

_____

_____

_____

_____

_____

Vocabulary

This section may be used to introduce or reinforce any mathematical words or phrases.

_____

_____

_____

_____

_____

_____

Go Figure

Name_____ Period_____ Date_____

● ●

Think — Read and analyze.

Susan's drive to her grandmother's house took $\frac{5}{6}$ of an hour. How many minutes did she drive? _____

Problem-solving plan...

Read			
Key words			
Analyze			
Add			
Subtract			
Multiply			
Divide			
Compare/ check			

Solve — Show and label your work here.

_____

_____

_____

_____

_____

_____

_____

_____

_____

_____

Communicate — Explain the strategies and thinking processes used to solve the problem(s).

_____

_____

_____

_____

Vocabulary

This section may be used to introduce or reinforce any mathematical words or phrases.

_____

_____

_____

_____

_____

_____

Go Figure

Name_____ Period_____ Date_____

Think Read and analyze.

Solve these problems using both regular math and algebra.

A. Soft drinks are packaged 12 cans to a box. There are 10 boxes to a case. There are 1,500 people at a basketball game. How many cases are needed to provide 75% of the people at the game with 2 soft drinks apiece? Round your answer to the next whole number. _____

B. What was the amount of profit if the soft drinks were purchased for $36.00 a case and sold for 50¢ a can and all but 10 cans were sold? _____

Problem-solving plan...

Read			
Key words			
Analyze			
Add			
Subtract			
Multiply			
Divide			
Compare/ check			

Solve Show and label your work here.

Communicate Explain the strategies and thinking processes used to solve the problem(s).

Vocabulary

round (*v*)—Express as the nearest whole number (5.62 rounds to 6).

profit—The amount of money gained in excess of the original cost.

algebra—An area of mathematics that uses symbols (such as letters) to explore relationships among numbers.

Go Figure

Name_____ Period_____ Date_____

Think   Read and analyze.

Pythagorean theorem: In a right triangle, the sum of the
squares of the legs (a and b) equals the square of the
hypotenuse (c): $a^2 + b^2 = c^2$.
Therefore, $c^2 - a^2 = b^2$ and $c^2 - b^2 = a^2$.

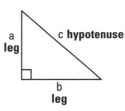

Problem-solving plan...

Read		
Key words		
Analyze		
Add		
Subtract		
Multiply		
Divide		
Compare/check		

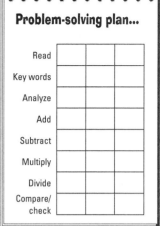

A. In a right triangle, what is the relationship between
the lengths of the legs and the length of the
hypotenuse? _____

_____

_____

_____

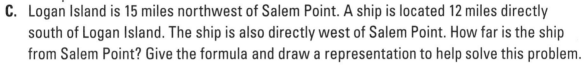

B. What is the length of the hypotenuse in △QRS? _____

C. Logan Island is 15 miles northwest of Salem Point. A ship is located 12 miles directly
south of Logan Island. The ship is also directly west of Salem Point. How far is the ship
from Salem Point? Give the formula and draw a representation to help solve this problem.

_____

Solve   Show and label your work here.

_____

_____

_____

_____

_____

_____

Communicate   Explain the strategies and thinking processes
used to solve the problem(s).

_____

_____

_____

_____

_____

_____

Vocabulary

theorem—A statement of
truth or an idea that can be
proved.

Pythagorean theorem—A
statement of truth discovered
by Pythagoras, a Greek
mathematician born about
500 B.C.

right triangle—A triangle that
has one right angle (90°).

leg—One of the two sides of
a right triangle that form the
right angle.

hypotenuse—The longest
side of a right triangle. It is
opposite the right angle.

square (*v*)—To multiply a
number by itself (3^2 means
$3 \times 3 = 9$; 5^2 means $5 \times 5 = 25$).

representation—A picture
that shows a mathematical
idea or relationship.

formula—A recipe or
equation used to solve a
mathematical problem.

Go Figure

Name_____ Period_____ Date_____

Think Read and analyze.

A. On the last weekly math quiz, José answered 34 of 40 questions correctly. What percent of the problems did he get right? _____

B. The final math exam had 80 questions on it. José gave the correct answer to 72 of the questions. His teacher used a grading scale in which F = below 60%, D = 60%–69%, C = 70%–79%, B = 80%–89%, and A = 90%–100%. What grade did José receive on his final exam? _____

Problem-solving plan...

Read			
Key words			
Analyze			
Add			
Subtract			
Multiply			
Divide			
Compare/ check			

Solve Show and label your work here.

Communicate Explain the strategies and thinking processes used to solve the problem(s).

Vocabulary

percent—One part of a whole that has been divided into 100 equal parts.

Go Figure

Name_____ Period_____ Date_____

Think   Read and analyze.

A diver is 125 feet below the surface of the ocean and rises 32 feet.

A. How deep is the diver now? _____

B. How many more feet must the diver rise to be 30 feet below the surface?

_____

Problem-solving plan...

Read			
Key words			
Analyze			
Add			
Subtract			
Multiply			
Divide			
Compare/ check			

Solve   Show and label your work here.

Communicate   Explain the strategies and thinking processes used to solve the problem(s).

Vocabulary

This section may be used to introduce or reinforce any mathematical words or phrases.

_____

_____

_____

_____

_____

_____

Try This!

Go Figure

Name_____ Period_____ Date_____

Think and Solve   Read and analyze.

Use the grid below to draw a figure that shows 64 as a square number.

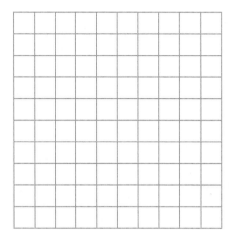

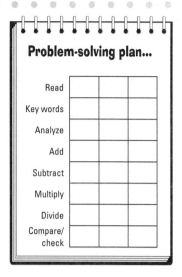

Problem-solving plan...

Read			
Key words			
Analyze			
Add			
Subtract			
Multiply			
Divide			
Compare/ check			

Communicate   Explain the strategies and thinking processes used to solve the problem(s).

_____

_____

_____

_____

_____

_____

Vocabulary

This section may be used to introduce or reinforce any mathematical words or phrases.

_____

_____

_____

_____

_____

_____

Go Figure

Name_____ Period_____ Date_____

Read and analyze.

Ten years ago the average price of a movie date, including popcorn and drinks, was $14.00. Today the average price is $32.20. What is the percent of increase in the cost of a movie date? _____

Problem-solving plan...

Read			
Key words			
Analyze			
Add			
Subtract			
Multiply			
Divide			
Compare/ check			

Solve **Show and label your work here.**

Communicate **Explain the strategies and thinking processes used to solve the problem(s).**

Vocabulary

percent—One part of a whole that has been divided into 100 equal parts.

Go Figure

Name_____ Period_____ Date_____

● ●

Think   Read and analyze.

The Carter family planned to take a family vacation to Mexico. The trip, including transportation, hotels, and food, would cost $5,280. They had two options for payment. Option 1: They could pay the full amount ahead of time by cash or check. Option 2: They could pay $1,500 down and $245 a month for 18 months.

A. Which option costs less? _____

B. How much is saved by choosing this option? _____

C. Underline any information in the problem that does not contribute to its solution.

Problem-solving plan...

Read			
Key words			
Analyze			
Add			
Subtract			
Multiply			
Divide			
Compare/check			

Solve   Show and label your work here.

Communicate   Explain the strategies and thinking processes used to solve the problem(s).

Vocabulary

option—Choice.

Go Figure

Name_____ Period_____ Date_____

Think and Solve   Read and analyze.

A. From the graph, what is the relationship between the number of hardware items sold and the amount of profit? _____

_____

B. What is the profit on each item? _____

C. How many items have to be sold to make a profit of $50? _____

D. What is the profit on 100 items? _____

E. On the graph, show the relationship between the amount of profit and the number of items sold when the profit on each item is $3.00 and 25 items are sold.

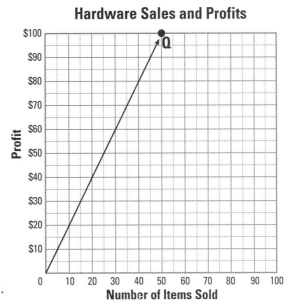

Hardware Sales and Profits

Problem-solving plan...

Read			
Key words			
Analyze			
Add			
Subtract			
Multiply			
Divide			
Compare/ check			

Communicate   Explain the strategies and thinking processes used to solve the problem(s).

_____

_____

_____

_____

_____

_____

_____

_____

Vocabulary

graph (*n*)—A visual representation of information or data.

relationship—The connection between identified variables.

horizontal axis—The scale on the bottom of a graph.

vertical axis—The scale on the left side of a graph.

profit—The amount of money gained in excess of original cost.

Go Figure

Name_____ Period_____ Date_____

Think   Read and analyze.

A. Give the formula for the volume of a cylinder. _____

B. The dimensions of a cylindrical gasoline tank are radius 7″ and height 30″. If there are 231 cubic inches in a gallon, how many gallons of gasoline will the tank hold? Use 3.14 for π.

_____

Problem-solving plan...

Read			
Key words			
Analyze			
Add			
Subtract			
Multiply			
Divide			
Compare/ check			

Solve   Show and label your work here.

Communicate   Explain the strategies and thinking processes used to solve the problem(s).

Vocabulary

dimension—A measurement, especially of height, width, or length.

cylindrical—Having the shape of a cylinder.

radius—A line segment from the center point of a circle to any point on the circle (half the length of the diameter).

height—The distance from the base to the top.

cubic—Having the volume and shape of a cube.

gallon—A liquid measure equal to four quarts.

Go Figure

Name_____ Period_____ Date_____

Read and analyze.

A. The temperature in the Arctic has been known to fall to –120° Fahrenheit, while temperatures in Death Valley can reach 125° F. What is the range between these two temperatures? _____

B. The range between two temperatures is 95° F. The low temperature is –21° F. What is the high temperature? _____

Problem-solving plan...

Read			
Key words			
Analyze			
Add			
Subtract			
Multiply			
Divide			
Compare/ check			

Solve **Show and label your work here.**

Communicate **Explain the strategies and thinking processes used to solve the problem(s).**

Vocabulary

Fahrenheit—A temperature scale that registers the freezing point of water at 32° F and the boiling point at 212° F.

range—The difference between the greatest and least values in a set of numerical data.

138 Try This!

Go Figure

Name_____ Period_____ Date_____

Think   Read and analyze.

A. Give the formulas for the area of a square and the area of a circle. _____

_____

B. John drew a circle in a 3-inch square. His drawing looked like this. How much of the square was not part of the circle? Use 3.14 for π.

_____

3″

3″

Problem-solving plan...

Read			
Key words			
Analyze			
Add			
Subtract			
Multiply			
Divide			
Compare/ check			

Solve   Show and label your work here.

Communicate   Explain the strategies and thinking processes used to solve the problem(s).

Vocabulary

This section may be used to introduce or reinforce any mathematical words or phrases.

_____

_____

_____

_____

_____

_____

Go Figure

Name_____ Period_____ Date_____

Think   Read and analyze.

There were 820 people at the convention center. A count was made of the number of people in each of the center's three conference rooms. There were 275 people in room A and 155 more people in room B than in room C. How many people were there in room B? _____

Problem-solving plan...

Read			
Key words			
Analyze			
Add			
Subtract			
Multiply			
Divide			
Compare/ check			

Solve   Show and label your work here.

Communicate   Explain the strategies and thinking processes used to solve the problem(s).

Vocabulary

This section may be used to introduce or reinforce any mathematical words or phrases.

_____
_____
_____
_____
_____
_____

Go Figure

Name_____ Period_____ Date_____

Think **Read and analyze.**

Guido and his friends are challenging each other with basic algebra problems. These are two of the problems they came up with.

A. The sum of two consecutive integers is 105. What are the integers? _____

B. The sum of three consecutive integers is 30. What are the integers?_____

C. Check the answers.

Problem-solving plan...

Read			
Key words			
Analyze			
Add			
Subtract			
Multiply			
Divide			
Compare/ check			

Solve **Show and label your work here.**

Communicate **Explain the strategies and thinking processes used to solve the problem(s).**

Vocabulary

algebra—An area of mathematics that uses symbols (such as letters) to explore relationships among numbers.

sum—The answer to an addition problem.

consecutive—Following each other in a sequential pattern.

integer—One of the set of whole numbers, their opposites, and 0 (... −2, −1, 0, 1, 2 ...).

Go Figure

Name_____ Period_____ Date_____

Think   Read and analyze.

A. William earned $7.75 per hour working at the mall. His gross pay
amounted to $310.00. How many hours did William work? _____

B. His net pay was $263.50. What percentage was his tax rate? _____

Problem-solving plan...

Read			
Key words			
Analyze			
Add			
Subtract			
Multiply			
Divide			
Compare/ check			

Solve   Show and label your work here.

Communicate   Explain the strategies and thinking processes used to solve
the problem(s).

Vocabulary

gross pay—Total pay before deductions.

net pay—Amount of pay received after deductions (taxes, social security, etc.).

percent—One part of a whole that has been divided into 100 equal parts.

Go Figure

Name_____ Period_____ Date_____

Read and analyze.

A. Sue, Raul, Toni, and Ali all invested in stocks in the 1990s. While the market was doing well, their stocks made significant gains. Sue's stock rose by $250.00, Raul's rose by $186.75, Toni's gained $132.00, and Ali's stock went up $170.25. What is the average amount of increase of their stocks?

_____

B. If Raul's investment increased by 6%, what was his original investment? _____

Problem-solving plan...

Read			
Key words			
Analyze			
Add			
Subtract			
Multiply			
Divide			
Compare/check			

Solve **Show and label your work here.**

Communicate **Explain the strategies and thinking processes used to solve the problem(s).**

Vocabulary

stock—Shares of ownership in a business.

invest—To buy shares of ownership in a business.

average—The sum of the values of a set of items divided by the number of items.

Go Figure

Name_____ Period_____ Date_____

The slope of a line tells how sharply the line is inclining. Slope is expressed as a ratio between the vertical change in y and the corresponding horizontal change in x. The formula is

$$\text{slope} = \frac{\text{change in y}}{\text{change in x}} \quad \text{OR} \quad \text{slope} = \frac{\text{rise}}{\text{run}}$$

Slope is always expressed as a fraction.

A. Graph the following points on the coordinate plane and draw a line through them: A (−2, 8) and B (6, 2); and C (8, 8) and D (−4, 2)

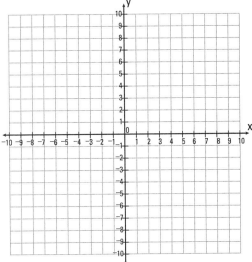

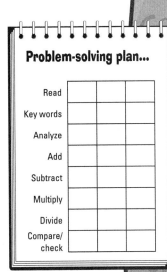

Problem-solving plan...

Read			
Key words			
Analyze			
Add			
Subtract			
Multiply			
Divide			
Compare/ check			

B. Find the slope of each line by selecting two points on the lines. Use the points given in question A and apply the formula.

$$\text{slope} = \frac{\text{change in y}}{\text{change in x}}$$

Vocabulary

slope—A number that describes the incline of a line.

incline—The slope, or slant, of a line.

ratio—A way of expressing a comparison between two numbers. The expression may be in three forms: 7:4 or $\frac{7}{4}$ or 7 to 4.

vertical—Rising upright from a level surface.

horizontal—Parallel to the horizon.

formula—A recipe or equation used to solve a mathematical problem.

graph (*v*)—To make a visual representation of information or data.

coordinate plane—A set of perpendicular number lines that intersect at their zero points, or origin. The horizontal line is labeled the x-axis and the vertical line is labeled the y-axis.

_____

_____

_____

_____

Try This!

Go Figure

Name_____ Period_____ Date_____

Read and analyze.

Solve these basic algebra problems.

A. The sum of two consecutive odd integers is 32. What are the integers? _____

B. The sum of two consecutive even integers is 66. What are the integers? _____

Problem-solving plan...

Read			
Key words			
Analyze			
Add			
Subtract			
Multiply			
Divide			
Compare/ check			

Solve **Show and label your work here.**

Communicate **Explain the strategies and thinking processes used to solve the problem(s).**

Vocabulary

This section may be used to introduce or reinforce any mathematical words or phrases.

_____

_____

_____

_____

_____

Go Figure

Name_____ Period_____ Date_____

Think · Read and analyze.

Darin has a savings account that pays 6% interest. The interest for one year amounted to $42.

A. How much did Darin have in his account at the beginning of the year?

_____

B. How much did he have after the interest was added to his account?

_____

C. How much more would he have had if the interest rate had been 6.5%?

_____

Problem-solving plan...

Read			
Key words			
Analyze			
Add			
Subtract			
Multiply			
Divide			
Compare/ check			

Solve · Show and label your work here.

Communicate · Explain the strategies and thinking processes used to solve the problem(s).

Vocabulary

interest—The amount paid for the use of money.

Go Figure

Name_____ Period_____ Date_____

Think Read and analyze.

The tenth grade class needed to raise $10,000 for a trip to Washington, D.C. After 12 days, they had raised 38% of the money needed for the trip. How much more money do they need to raise?

_____

Problem-solving plan...

Read			
Key words			
Analyze			
Add			
Subtract			
Multiply			
Divide			
Compare/ check			

Solve Show and label your work here.

Communicate Explain the strategies and thinking processes used to solve the problem(s).

Vocabulary

percent—One part of a whole that has been divided into 100 equal parts.

Go Figure

Name_____ Period_____ Date_____

Think and Solve Read and analyze.

A. Classify these triangles by their sides and their angles.

Classification by sides: Classification by angles:
  isosceles   obtuse
  equilateral   acute
  scalene   right

1.

2.

3.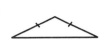

4.

_____ _____ _____ _____

5.

6.

7.

8.

_____ _____ _____ _____

9.

10.

11.

12.

_____ _____ _____ _____

B. Draw, name, and define an equilateral, isosceles, and scalene triangle.

1.   **2.**

_____   _____

_____   _____

_____   _____

    3.

_____

_____

_____

Communicate Explain the strategies and thinking processes used to solve the problem(s).

_____

_____

_____

_____

_____

Vocabulary

triangle—A two-dimensional closed figure that has three sides and three angles.

isosceles triangle—A triangle that has two congruent sides.

scalene triangle—A triangle that has no congruent sides.

equilateral triangle—A triangle that has three congruent sides.

obtuse triangle—A triangle that has an obtuse angle (greater than 90°).

acute triangle—A triangle that has three acute angles (less than 90°).

right triangle—A triangle that has one right angle (90°).

Go Figure

Name_____ Period_____ Date_____

Think and Solve Read and analyze.

A. Graph and label the following points:

A (0, −4) and B (4, −1)
C (1, 4) and D (0, 1)
W (3, 2) and X (3, −1)
P (2, 2) and Q (6, 4)

B. Draw a line connecting each set of points.

C. Using the formula for slope, calculate the slope of each line.

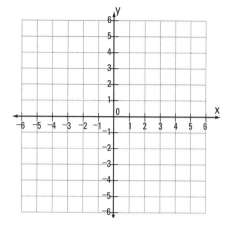

Problem-solving plan...

Read			
Key words			
Analyze			
Add			
Subtract			
Multiply			
Divide			
Compare/ check			

Communicate Explain the strategies and thinking processes used to solve the problem(s).

Vocabulary

set—A collection of objects or numbers.

graph (*v*)—To make a visual representation of information or data.

slope—A number that describes the incline of a line.

formula—A recipe or equation used to solve a mathematical problem.

Go Figure

Name_____ Period_____ Date_____

Think   Read and analyze.

Roxie and her friends wrote some math problems. Can you solve them?

A. A high school science class has 5 more girls than boys. The total number of students in the class is 23. How many girls are there? _____ How many boys? _____

B. What number when multiplied by 9 and decreased by 9 is 72? _____

Problem-solving plan...

Read			
Key words			
Analyze			
Add			
Subtract			
Multiply			
Divide			
Compare/ check			

Solve   Show and label your work here.

Communicate   Explain the strategies and thinking processes used to solve the problem(s).

Vocabulary

decrease—To become less or smaller.

Try This!

Go Figure

Name_____ Period_____ Date_____

Think   Read and analyze.

Elena's aunt's age is 13 years less than 5 times Elena's age. Elena is 10 years old. How old is her aunt? _____

Problem-solving plan...

Read			
Key words			
Analyze			
Add			
Subtract			
Multiply			
Divide			
Compare/ check			

Solve   Show and label your work here.

Communicate   Explain the strategies and thinking processes used to solve the problem(s).

Vocabulary

This section may be used to introduce or reinforce any mathematical words or phrases.

_____

_____

_____

_____

_____

_____

Vocabulary/Index by Lesson Number